"Artificial intelligence ... approach to contact da... **Powered by DiscoverOr...**

"Whether you are a sales manager or a seller, sales tools powered by AI can enhance and improve how you perform the most important parts of your job. From building a target list to engaging with prospects as a seller to forecasting, training, and coaching as a manager, we have so many tools available today. Selling and leading sales without the aid of AI is like fighting with one arm tied behind your back." **Matthew McDarby, Managing Director, Specialized Sales Systems**

"Every Industry is getting more crowded and competitive; everyone is looking for an edge. Data is growing at an exponential growth rate. Those who can harness this data and turn it into actionable insights will be the ones who thrive. Automation and AI provide the infrastructure to make this possible." **Babar Batla, CEO, SalesDirector.ai**

"Chad Burmeister is a thought leader who understands the future of AI from a sales perspective. While many people look at AI with a skeptical eye, fearing for their jobs, this book will serve as your guide to a future filled with new possibilities for creating more customers, accelerating the sales cycle, saving hundreds of hours of research time and moving ahead of your competition. A must read if you want to future proof your sales organization. Well written, a fast read for the busy, action-oriented sales leader." **Gerhard Gschwandtner, CEO, SellingPower Magazine**

"In Sales, Time Kills Deals, in Modern Sales AI Kills Time!" **Joël Le Bon, Ph.D., Marketing & Sales Professor, Johns Hopkins University, Carey Business School**

"If you're not using AI for sales, you are putting your organization at a disadvantage in today's crowded marketplace." **David McClean, Managing Partner, SDR Systems Group**

"With the advent of big data, and artificial intelligence, companies can now leverage artificial intelligence to ensure that companies hire the right sales professionals who both "can sell" and "will sell" and that they have the right reps and leaders in their existing sales team." **Lori Richardson, CEO, Score More Sales**

"This is a great read and full of information any sales leader serious about wanting to improve their craft. Chad continues to produce valuable tools and content to stay up to date on all things sales, AI uses in the Sales Stack that benefits those involved in Inside sales." **Cheryl Christensen, CEO, Data2Develop**

"AI-powered talent science is now revealing the unique combination of attributes that predict A-Player performance in specific sales role. This is generating tremendous new business value previously hidden from sales leaders and recruiters using cookie cutter assessments. Chad Burmeister's seminal book is similarly adding new value to a field set to have a dominating influence on how the world does business." **Brett Morris, CEO and Co-Founder, PerceptionPredict®**

AI FOR SALES:

HOW ARTIFICIAL INTELLIGENCE IS CHANGING SALES

Chad Burmeister

www.ScaleX.ai

chad@scalex.ai

CONTENTS

Acknowledgments

This book is dedicated to my children—Brendan and Brianna Burmeister—without them, life would not be nearly as fulfilling as it is; to my wife Tracey Burmeister, who puts up with my sh*t; and to God, the father and creator—without God, my life and work would be utterly meaningless.

Dedication

This book is dedicated to every sales leader that I've ever worked for — Philip Ragatz, Leonard Mongiello, Stephen D'Angelo, Kris Duggan, Kevin Hadad, Bobby Jaffari, Mitch Tarica, MJ Shutte, Travis Patterson, Jim Reiss, Stu Schmidt, Chris Beall, John Raedar, Faiza Hughell, and more ... your leadership and belief in me as a sales professional has made all the difference in me becoming the sales leader that I am today.

Foreword

Sales has changed more in the past five years than in the past fifty. As we know, change is permanent. However, the speed and scope of change today is different. Mathematicians call it the third derivative or the rate of the increase in acceleration; and *increase in acceleration* is exactly what Artificial Intelligence (AI) is bringing to modern sales.

Chad Burmeister understands change, modern sales, and AI. As sales executives embrace the fast-moving era of digital transformation, they need to understand *why* and *how* AI is affecting the sales environment. They will find pragmatic answers in Chad's book on AI for Sales.

Why AI is affecting sales? AI is impacting sales because data nourishes AI, and sales is about data. In fact, the future of sales is about data science. But when it comes to AI, it's all about data quality. Chad right away and rightfully addresses this critical issue in the first chapter, and explains why poor data costs companies hundreds of thousands of dollars per year and loss in revenue. Throughout the chapters, the reader also quickly understands why sales is the perfect field of growth for AI. Indeed, because sales comprises a wide array of administrative and time consuming tasks, AI can do the work better, while allowing sales representatives to also do the work better, i.e., having more productive conversations with the customers. Nevertheless, in the world of AI for Sales the very role of salespeople will be redefined.

This leads to the fascinating question of *how AI is affecting sales.* As a professor, I value education and clarification, and thus would like to commend Chad on his methodology to approach such a question. Since the sales stack contains over

600 hundred sales technologies, making clarification of relevant technologies virtually impossible, Chad leverages the Vendor Neutral Certified 100 Landscape and 20 categories to analyze how AI impacts sales in each of these areas. By simply and methodologically structuring the book's chapters around Vendor Neutral's 20 categories Chad not only demonstrates how AI is changing every aspect of the sales environment, but also shows how AI transcends modern sales. Yet, he does not stop there. Each category features a specific technology and examples often from experts in the field and envisions the future of AI for Sales.

This book is necessary, pragmatic, and bold. Just like what Chad is bringing to modern sales. The reader will take away the AI for Sales' *nice-to-have* and *need-to-have* for today, and tomorrow. But more importantly, Chad's book will certainly encourage more debate and a better understanding of the speed and scope of change in sales, for the good. In fact, *in Sales, Time Kills Deals, in Modern Sales AI Kills Time!*

Joël Le Bon, Ph.D.
Marketing & Sales Professor
Faculty Director for Leadership in Digital Marketing & Sales Transformation
Johns Hopkins University, Carey Business School

What is *AI for Sales*?

Artificial intelligence for sales is a term that came into existence in January of 2019 when Gabe Larsen, VP of Growth at InsideSales.com, made the claim in a LinkedIn post and video that artificial intelligence would not displace sales development representatives, but it would actually empower them to schedule more appointments.

100,000 "likes" and over 300 comments later, the AI *for* sales debate was shaped. This book defines what artificial intelligence for sales is, and the impact that it is having on sales.

AI for sales can be misconstrued and used by companies to promote their brands in misleading ways. We'll use the Wikipedia definition of artificial intelligence + sales to define what artificial intelligence for sales is.

Artificial intelligence (Wikipedia definition): In computer science, artificial intelligence (AI), sometimes called machine intelligence, is intelligence demonstrated by machines, in contrast to the natural intelligence displayed by humans and animals.

Sales (Wikipedia definition): Activities related to selling.

Artificial intelligence for sales: Machine intelligence demonstrated by machines leveraged to perform activities related to selling.

The Vendor Neutral Certified 100 Landscape

In 2017, Vendor Neutral launched the Vendor Neutral Certified 100 Landscape to help business leaders better understand the alternatives in sales technology so that they didn't have to research the 600+ sales technologies that are being offered in the marketplace.

In this book, we leverage the Vendor Neutral Certified 100 Landscape to categorize the sales tech stack and expand on how companies are leveraging artificial intelligence in each of these areas—focused on actual use cases today, and the future use cases of tomorrow.

Vendor Neutral Certified 100 (www.vendorneutral.com)

The Vendor Neutral Certified 100 categories

1. Lead / list building
2. Pricing and configuration
3. Scheduling
4. Quota and territory management
5. Account targeting and go-to market
6. Prospect engagement
7. Sales enablement / content management
8. Outbound prospecting / agent-assisted
9. Account and opportunity planning / management
10. Video selling
11. Lead engagement
12. eSignature
13. Sales assessments
14. Mobile selling and content engagement
15. Sales compensation
16. Knowledge sharing
17. Conversation intelligence
18. Skills development and reinforcement
19. Sales training content
20. Customer value management for sales

Artificial intelligence is already having an impact on each of these categories, and, in this book, we'll share how.

Chapter 1:

Lead / List Building

Welcome to ground zero: your lead list. Yep, artificial intelligence (AI) is uprooting every part of the sales process, all the way down to the foundation — your sales contact data, or **sales intelligence (https://discoverorg.com/blog/sales-intelligence-power/)**.

For accurate, actionable results, AI needs good data — and lots of it. High-performing teams are five times more likely to be using AI than underperforming sales teams, according to Salesforce. A foundation of good data allows artificial intelligence to generate robust, accurate insights.

And that begins with the lead list.

Suppose you have a list of 50,000 names. In the past, salespeople would have sent an email to all 50,000 people and hoped they would self-identify interest by responding to the email.

"Artificial intelligence adds a more sophisticated, targeted approach to **contact data (https://discoverorg.com/),**" says ZoomInfo Powered by DiscoverOrg CEO Henry Schuck. "With AI embedded in the process, sales teams can score accounts and build lists quickly, knowing that the account will be a good fit for their product. They can be confident that the right contact is on the line before any email is ever sent."

AI may consider scoring factors that you already use, such as company size, location, or budget cycle. But artificial intelligence can also find underlying patterns and commonalities in the data that humans would not notice. For example, AI might identify considerations like the prospect's place in the org chart; seasonality; or the company's budget cycle, installed technologies, stage of growth, or other factors you've never thought of—all of which might impact a prospect's likelihood to buy!

In addition to uncovering valuable insights, artificial intelligence can work with datasets that are too large for humans to manage.

More than just determining whether accounts are likely to be good fits for your product, artificial intelligence also makes that lead list a lot warmer on the individual contact level.

Without AI-generated insights, that plain old lead list is ice-cold—and not in the refreshing beverage way. Salespeople spend their time hunting for a good contact at the account, hunting for a direct phone number and guessing at an email address, hunting for background information and social media context ... if they're lucky. When that information isn't available, they must navigate the company phone tree, trying to cold-call someone able to make purchase decisions.

This is a lot of time spent not selling! Artificial intelligence solves this problem by serving up insights that can warm the call.

These efficiencies in list-building and prospecting have a serious downstream impact on the rest of the sales process! With 200+ ZoomInfo Powered by DiscoverOrg data points on every company, our customers grow four times faster than the S&P 500, on average.

"Before good, AI-enabled data," says Eddie Baron, Head of Global Account Development at Gameffective, "our lead generation had been mostly inbound-focused with PPC. There was hardly any way to guarantee the quality of a lead." With accurate data and AI insights from a tool like ZoomInfo Powered by DiscoverOrg, **Gameffective cut research sales time in half** (**https://discoverorg.com/resource/case-study-gameffective/**) and boost productivity by 17%!

"Now we can invite the right people, the people who are far more relevant, far more interested, and far more likely to convert."

It will never be possible to predict human behavior—or buying behavior—with perfect accuracy. Sales conversion rates will never be 100%. But rapid advancements in artificial intelligence, combined with the large volume of available data needed for accurate results, offer a far more effective way of growing sales pipeline and revenue.

Featured Technology: Lead / List Building

 zoominfo
Powered by DiscoverOrg

In 2015, when I was Senior Director of Global Sales Development for RingCentral tasked with optimizing an inbound SDR team, while launching an outbound BDR team, my first project within the first 90 days was to bring in ZoomInfo Powered by DiscoverOrg.

For companies like RingCentral who rely on penetrating target accounts, there is no other viable solution on the market besides ZoomInfo Powered by DiscoverOrg. Why? Because only ZoomInfo can claim a 97% or higher direct dial coverage on data. And companies who prospect most effectively leverage not just digital communications (email and social) but also phone outreach.

If you use any other provider besides ZoomInfo, you will quickly realize that direct dial phone numbers matter. If it takes 20 attempts to talk to someone on a list, or 40 attempts, that may not sound like a big deal, but IT IS A BIG DEAL. It takes an average sales person 2 hours to make 20 phone dials. Bad data literally costs companies hundreds of thousands of dollars per year in low productivity of their workforce, and lost revenue.

Lead / List Building

Imagine a new sales professional joins a company. In the past, getting the leads transferred into CRM, territory changes, and the configuration of all of the technologies used for outreach was a total mess.

Now, imagine a new sales professional joins your company, and they get automated access to the flow of leads, powered by an intelligent list builder that uses artificial intelligence to track signals, score leads, and automate the list building process to be the most optimal list of targets to reach out to. Take it one step further, now a virtual assistant sends the email, tracks the opens, clicks, and replies, and even responds to the prospect. That's already happening at the time of the writing of this book.

In 2018, a ScaleX.ai client in the telecommunications space leveraged a list provider (that was *not* powered by AI or intent data) to generate a list of ~18,000 contacts. 169,858 sales activities were completed against this list to generate 102 meetings, and 206 future meetings.

In 2019, the same ScaleX.ai client is leveraging intent data from Bombora and, rather than investing ~$200,000 to drive 169,858 sales activities to a list of 18,000 random leads, they will be monitoring the intent across 1.5M companies to determine when and whom to reach out to. The expected outcome is two to three times more meetings.

Chapter 2:

Pricing and Configuration

Proposify and SPARXiQ (formerly SPA & SPASIGMA) are two of the Vendor Neutral Certified 100 companies in the 2018 Landscape.

Other technologies in this space include Qwilr, PandaDoc, Conga, RFPIO, RFP360, DocSend, Quoteworks, and more. **G2 Crowd** offers an expansive coverage of the space.

G2 Grid® for **Proposal**

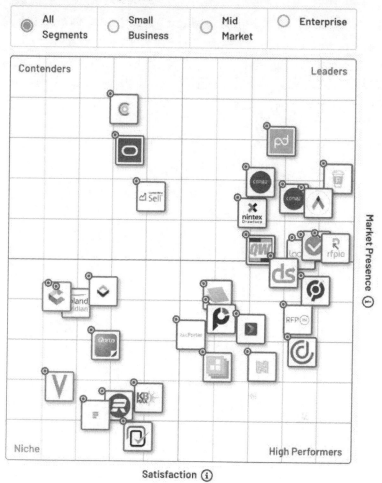

According to G2 Crowd, proposal software is designed to streamline and automate the proposal and request for proposal (RFP) process for sales operations. Sales professionals benefit from proposal software features like the ability to quickly generate documents in multiple file formats, share documents through multiple channels, and track the impact of RFP and proposal documents on the sales success.

Proposals can be the first important step in a business relationship, which means that salespeople need to include valuable and consistent content that is personalized to customer profiles and needs. Proposal tools are usually used to help sales or partnerships, so common integrations include CRM software, CPQ software, e-signature software, and accounting software.

Featured Technology: Pricing and Configuration

According to the Qwilr website, Qwilr quickly creates beautiful and intuitive proposals and sales & marketing documents. And, from ScaleX.ai experiences using Qwilr for semi-automated proposal writing, it does a lot more than just that.

In the first ninety days of launching ScaleX.ai, and then BDR.ai later in the year, creating a set of SKUs (officially known as a stock-keeping unit) can be difficult, especially when half of the company is a services company and the other half is a product/SaaS company. To solve this challenge, ScaleX.ai turned to Qwilr. So now, rather than creating a brand new proposal each and every time the sales team has a conversation, they simply create an opportunity in SalesForce.com, pick a proposal template, and then make a few minor modifications via the Qwilr proposal technology.

Step 1: Choose a template

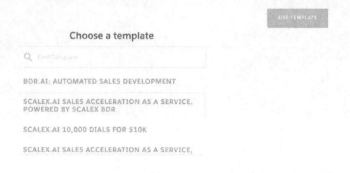

Step 2: Edit the template

Step 3: Make sure to use video in your proposals

Step 4: eSignature makes it simple for clients to sign-up

SCALEX.AI **INVESTMENT**

By "accepting" this quote below, client agrees to the ScaleX Master
Services Agreement (MSA), and the products and services listed in
this Statement of Work (SOW)

Design				$2,500.00
Description	**Item**	**Quantity**		**Price**
Kick-Off Call (~60 minutes)				
Implementation & Playbook Design (~8 hours)	$2500	1	Day	$2,500.00
Optional - Data (5,000 Records w/Phone & Email)	$3000	0	Unit	$0.00

Deliver				$37,500.00
Description	**Item**	**Quantity**		**Price**
Sales Acceleration as a Service. 90,000 Sales Activities in 3 months including a mix of Phone Dials (~15,000), Email, and LinkedIn Outreach (includes up to 8 hours of BDR Coaching)	SALES ACCELERA...	1	QUART...	$37,500.00

TOTAL EXCLUDING TAX	$40,000.00
Total	**$40,000.00**

Pricing and Configuration

Imagine a sales rep talking to a client via Zoom Video, enabling Chorus to capture the conversation through Conversation Intelligence, and then having the AI, with human oversight, configure the proposal using a solution like Proposify or Qwilr.

Now imagine your team has strategic pricing data from a company like SPARXiQ (formerly SPA & SPASIGMA) and the cost to serve your customers in one report. Your salespeople will have the prescriptive actionable data they've been asking for. They will understand product groups that are sensitive to price—as well as those not historically price sensitive—from your transaction data in your ERP system.

Imagine your salespeople having average, good, and low-price data from your own sales team available to them in the CRM when they quote and the price they chose to sell each item for is tied to a specific compensation. For example, with data analytics, we can show the price range for each SKU and identify the lowest price, average price, and expert prices that that salesperson's peers have sold that SKU at previously.

The pricing managers are no longer seen as the bad guys to the sales team, raising prices and risking the loss of a customer. With transaction data analytics, the price manager is now able to provide actionable data sales wants and needs. Like what?

- Accounts showing signs your customers may be defecting, leaving you with what we refer to as high-risk clients

- Up sell opportunities – comparing your account to others like them

- Cross sell opportunities – suggesting items they are not buying but others like them are

- Sales reps can have actionable data dashboards for their accounts or region, and their manager can have one for their team

- Orders behind – using transaction data over a number of months, the salesperson will receive a list of items the customer should have bought by now—based on their history of transactions—but have not

- Low volume – snapshot of what items sales is not seeing at similar accounts

- Attrition analytics – accounts that have left over the last year and what their sales volume represented

- Target product mix score

- Share of wallet score

- Top line revenue by region, by account, and by item

- Sales representative training opportunities identified – for example, we have one price analytic tool that shows how your salespeople discount. Time and time again, we see salespeople discounting in round numbers, e.g., 10%, 15%, 20%. We can share a graphic illustration for each client.

This is a symptom which shows that the sales team needs a course like tactical negotiations skills where they will learn to use smaller discounts, such as 2.3%, 3.7% and so on.

Empowered with your own price data by item, for the first time sales will be able to know if a buyer saying they need a 30% discount is a want or a need.

Look at the price band data for this item in your price analytics history ... oh, interesting, not one person on your entire team has ever needed a 30% discount, but the average price we have consistently won business at has been a 12% discount. Think about the financial impact!

Proposals take sales professionals hours to write in many cases and, often, they are product centric and vary across the organization. There is a common phrase: **time kills deals**. Over and over again, we see data that reinforces that the longer you take to quote the smaller your closing rate is.

Analytics finally equips your team to make smart decisions (you've heard of *smart machines*, now it's the era of *smart sales*) based on market, region, product group, price sensitivity history, team prices sold data, and by SKU.

The power of AI for proposal writing — better proposals that articulate the client's needs and how the solution maps to those needs, the impact of not solving the need, and the impact of solving the need, with an ROI embedded in the proposal — is *automagically* powered by artificial intelligence.

The power of AI for your team is higher closing rates, more share of wallet, higher gross profit margins, giving the customers services they value, and eliminating the costs of service they do not value ... ultimately leading to more sales, more profits, and greater organic growth.

Chapter 3:

Scheduling

If you haven't discovered the power of automating the scheduling of meetings, then you are likely wasting hours of your life *(and equally important, your company's life)* that could be invested in more value-added work—there are better things to be doing than trying to coordinate schedules.

And, if you haven't integrated scheduling into your sales process, then you are most definitely leaving appointments, pipeline, and closed/won business on the table for your competition, which makes it easier for their customers to connect with them.

What is scheduling? Scheduling is enabling the customer or prospect to schedule time on your calendar that is convenient for them. By integrating your Outlook or Gmail calendar into a web-based application, you expose your availability and enable your prospects to book time with you. As a sales leader of over twenty years, I've deployed this technology multiple times, and it's a game changer.

Featured Technology: Scheduling

 timetrade®

There is a clear market leader in the Vendor Neutral Certified 100 space, and that's TimeTrade. TimeTrade was launched in 2000 and has since become the standard in online "intelligent appointment scheduling."

The business problem? In the absence of an online scheduling solution, it can take people upwards of 5-7 email exchanges to land on a meeting time, and that's when just two people are involved in the meeting. When a meeting requires three or more attendees, it can take days to finally schedule such a meeting that works for everyone, and then someone can't make the meeting, and it's back to the drawing board.

What Is Intelligent Appointment Scheduling?

Intelligent online appointment scheduling helps companies optimize engagement through all phases of the customer relationship—helping sales, marketing, and customer service & support teams in any industry to connect and engage with prospects, customers, and clients more quickly and easily than ever. Intelligent online appointment scheduling can be integrated into almost any channel, allowing prospects and customers to make meetings and appointments at the peak of their interest.

Placing a "schedule an appointment" button on an organization's website makes it easy for prospects and customers to schedule and confirm online appointments at their convenience. Enabled by artificial intelligence, these conversations deliver the personalized attention expected by today's on-demand consumers.

Scheduling

With the advent of bots and virtual assistants (that facilitate email exchange), calendaring is something that is becoming a *must have* in the sales process. Currently, calendar tools like TimeTrade enable the customer to book their own meeting. As AI for sales enters this space, what if AI could suggest others to attend the meeting? Maybe the buyer is low-level; could the AI suggest bringing in his or her boss? Is there a better time of day or day of the week for a closing call versus a discovery call or demo call? Could the AI actually suggest to the person who scheduled the meeting that they forward the invite to others?

Chapter 4:

Quota and Territory Management

During the writing of *AI for Sales*, it was announced that MapAnything (a pioneer in quota and territory management) would be acquired by SalesForce.com. This acquisition puts SalesForce.com in the data visualization space to provide customers with a map-based interface to uncover valuable insights and make data-driven insights for future growth.

Another solution provider in the quota and territory management space is CallidusCloud. CallidusCloud's Territory and Quota provides a simple way to plan territories and quotas, reducing cost and maximizing revenue. This end-to-end solution offers sales operations a collaborative way to align sales territories, calculate quotas, and distribute them to the field.

CallidusCloud customers can leverage rules to manage territories and a quota recommendation engine to set quotas automatically, based on forward-looking and backward-looking metrics. Customers can also easily distribute quotas across direct and indirect sales channels using productized top-down and bottom-up quota distribution.

Featured Technology:
Quota and Territory Management

On April 17, 2019, SalesForce.com acquired MapAnything for its location-based intelligence products, and for good reason. MapAnything, a Charlotte, NC-based intelligence software and services provider, offers a routing and scheduling engine, integrated GPS tracking capabilities, and a location-based workflow layer that helps answer "complex spatial questions" and driver prompter customer service.

MapAnything's Fortune 500 and Forbes Global 2,000 customers — which number 1,900 — span financial, manufacturing, and consumer packaging (CPG) industries including American Express, Lyft, Capital One, and more.

Quota and Territory Management

The future of quota and territory management software is likely a move away from point solutions to whole solutions, built into CRM and other applications.

Chapter 5:

Account Targeting and Go-To-Market

There are two companies in the Vendor Neutral Certified 100 landscape — InsideView Technologies and TechTarget. Both solutions offer a unique approach to account targeting. TechTarget focuses on driving better marketing performance by engaging with companies known to be in the market searching for technology solutions (similar to Bombora). InsideView helps customers manage data quality, discover new markets, and target and engage with the right buyers.

SiriusDecisions created the Demand Generation Waterfall® in 2006, and, over the years, it has evolved. In 2017, "Target Demand" was launched as a way to measure the top of the funnel marketing metrics.

Link to the article: **http://bit.ly/Sirius-Waterfall**

Traditionally, Sirius Decisions, and other leading analyst firms have focused on "active demand," so the shift to "target demand" has been significant.

The target demand stage definition is total addressable market (TAM). The number of target demand units that exist for the solution in the defined market. As a mentor used to say, "If it's not a list, then it can't be called a market."

Featured Technology:
Account Targeting and Go-To-Market

InsideView, founded in 2005, offers a targeting intelligence platform, built using artificial intelligence, to help businesses discover and visualize new market opportunities. InsideView also provides metrics to analyze and optimize market performance. With a surge of more data and systems, filtering the signals to cut through the noise is now a critical challenge to drive rapid revenue growth. With data expertise and best-in-class customer support, InsideView delivers the industry's most relevant and reliable buyer signals and is trusted by the world's best performing B2B companies.

In a recent conversation with Joe Andrews, VP Marketing at InsideView, and Joshua Nguyen, Director of Product Management at Data Platform, at InsideView, we learned a lot about how InsideView's customers use artificial intelligence to gain insights that inform go-to-market strategies. Artificial Intelligence is used to help identify their ideal customer profile (who are my perfect customers, where do they work, what do they do). The InsideView platform is built using machine learning to aggregate and standardize data from thousands of sources and validate accuracy at scale.

InsideView also delivers its AI algorithm within its products to provide customers with predictive insights that drive sales and marketing activity against their best opportunities. InsideView Apex helps customers define ICP and target markets, then align the operational systems and teams around the strategy, e.g., identifying 'best-fit' accounts that allow a company to target prospects within their total addressable market (TAM) that look like their best customers.

Screen shots from an InsideView executive briefing.

InsideView Apex:

Step 1: Map your existing customers and prospects against InsideView's external market data to understand and size your target addressable market (TAM), then analyze your market penetration, see white space opportunities, and export new accounts and contacts to execute targeted sales and marketing campaigns.

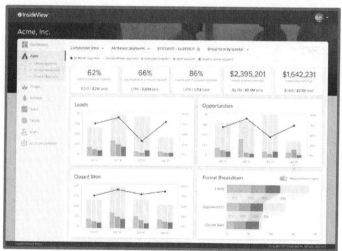

Step 2: Uncover additional look-alike accounts that closely match the characteristics of your ICPs, leveraging InsideView's AI-based predictive modeling.

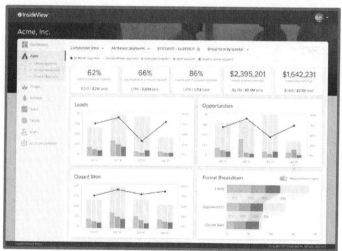

Step 3: Go from counting email click rates and measuring lead conversions to analyzing what really matters. Are you getting the right leads and opportunities? Are you closing deals with the right customers? Are you penetrating the markets that matter?

Account Targeting and Go-To-Market

At RingCentral, the Vice President of Global Sales and Services Operations, who joined the company in August of 2016, wasted no time mapping out the companies who were worth investing sales resources and time to sell into. Within 100 days of joining the company, he had created a master XLS with more than 100 columns that included things like the total number of available lines, growth rates, technologies deployed, and the like. And he had associated a score with each of these top 2000 – 3000 companies.

In my first meeting with him, he shared how, as VP of Global Sales Strategy for SalesForce.com, he helped them move to a similar model, where the top sales reps would focus on the accounts that could move the needle. So, rather than a rep owning 100 accounts, he said that he moved that down to the top 5-10 accounts for one sales team.

As this space continues to evolve, and AI for sales evolves, these algorithms and methodologies will make their way into solutions like those provided by InsideView.

Chapter 6:

Prospect Engagement

Since InsideSales.com achieved Unicorn status ($1B valuation), several technology players arrived on the market to take aim at the market leader, and they have been quite successful in doing so. Both Outreach.io and SalesLoft have also achieved similar market valuations and show no signs of slowing down *yet*.

Prospect Engagement is what it sounds like it is—a platform to engage with prospects, through multiple channels of outreach, whether the prospect comes in as a lead through marketing, is an outbound prospect, or an existing customer that should be engaged on a regular basis to drive cross-sell, up-sell, and renewals.

The Vendor Neutral Certified 100 players include SalesLoft, SmartCloud, Outreach, and VanillaSoft.

Featured Technology: Prospect Engagement

 scale^X.ai

ScaleX.ai is an interesting company because it doesn't have the proverbial handcuffs that a typical company has—because ScaleX partners with other tech companies to bring together a best-of-breed technology stack, powered by people, to deliver the best solutions for the best companies.

As a result of strategic alliances with best-of-breed companies, ScaleX has been able to pivot as the market changes and continually enhance the solution stack to over-deliver to customer requirements. For example, in the first 100 deployments, ScaleX saw a gap in the solution—many customers didn't have a messaging strategy. ScaleX Intelligent Messaging solves that.

Today, ScaleX.ai offers what will most likely become the more optimal route for many companies for years to come. Rather than hire a dedicated BDR to execute research, then phone, email, and social outreach, they will turn to companies like ScaleX.ai and BDR.ai to execute AI-powered messaging and 7X-20X more sales activities for the same investment.

The Virtual BDR solution

1. Use AI to understand the personality/buyer type of existing customers

2. Profile hundreds of influencers within target companies that match the buyer personality of client's best customers

3. Create up to 84 unique messages (LinkedIn, Email, Call Scripts) aligning the unique value proposition to the correct buyer personality

4. Execute ~25,000 sales activities (phone, email, and social) into these influencers in < 90 days

5. Typically, clients see 25 – 55 meetings during the first 90 days, and, more important, they close 200% more deals.

THE FUTURE

Prospect Engagement (Virtual Assistants)

From sitting "shotgun" in the front seat of AI for sales, this is my prediction of what will change in the next few years.

Change #1: The economy experiences a downturn leading to lay-offs and the need to optimize pipeline generation. Even if this doesn't happen, when competition uses AI for sales, it will force their competitor to do so.

Change #2: As a result of the economic downturn, companies still have to deliver to their sales targets and will be required to do more with less (fewer resources).

Change #3: As digital sales continue to consume real estate on your screen, and the bots take over this channel, human to human connections become more important than ever before.

Impact #1: Chatbots have already taken over for humans on nearly every B2B website. Companies like Intercom and Drift make it easy (and inexpensive) to program a bot to handle almost any question that the website visitor can dream up. This trend will continue with AI and Natural Language Processing (NLP).

Impact #2: Knowing that chatbots have been programmed using machine learning and artificial intelligence, this will spill over to email—for inbound lead follow-up (like Conversica and ScaleX.ai) and outbound (ScaleX.ai), and ultimately voice. My father-in-law received a call to his cell phone recently and interacted with what he thought was a human for five to ten minutes (this "person" was trying to get him to donate money to the local police department). He eventually found out that it wasn't a person he was talking to. It was a bot!

Impact #3: Now that the bots have taken over chat and email (and soon social), human-to-human phone conversations become more important than ever before. The difference is that now they will be powered by artificial intelligence. Companies like JOYai enable a sales professional with language to be used, tone of voice, and entire scripts, within the dialing application, to speak to the specific buyer type (by personality and buyer type). This is scary and exciting at the same time.

ScaleX has seen clients go from a few meetings per month to a few meetings per day by optimizing messaging (digital and phone) to convert more conversations into meetings.

The Virtual Assistants (chatbots, email, social) will be automated more and more. The human sales professional will be required to have more phone conversations powered by sales acceleration technology.

Chapter 7:

Sales Enablement and
Content Management

The Vendor Neutral Certified 100 contains more vendors in this category than any other. Yet the fundamental need most of these products address—how to find the most fitting piece of content for my prospect—has been superseded by a much more sophisticated one.

Today, companies must overcome customer and prospect fatigue, immunity to noise, and lack of engagement until it's too late to make an impact on the buyer's journey, especially given that anywhere from 57% to 81% of that journey happens prior to engagement with sales. The discussion is no longer about how to enable sales and how to manage content; it's about how to engage with your prospects effectively across the entire customer lifecycle, via all customer-facing functions, in a consistent manner.

Engaging with customers in today's market requires hyper-personalization; customers expect meaningful experiences on every channel. Achieving such hyper-personalization at scale requires extremely high-quality data and well-applied AI.

A recent **Forbes report** (http://bit.ly/ForbesPersonalizationReport) revealed that 40% of marketers have seen a direct impact on sales via personalization, yet less than half (41%) of their organizations view personalization as a high priority. Many enterprises still use the same generic website, email, or sales funnel for every single B2B interaction despite **Gartner's (https://blogs.gartner.com/noah-elkin/the-long-and-winding-road-to-real-time-marketing/)** observation that "organizations that have fully invested in all types of online personalization will outsell companies that have not by more than 30%."

What does it really mean? It simply isn't sufficient anymore to provide leads, playbooks, and supporting content, all separately, and then expect a massive improvement in results. Instead, here's what the most effective organizations are doing today:

- Marketing and sales enablement must come together and orchestrate Go-To-Market (GTM) motions where they provide leads/targets, AI based auto-personalized messaging, content, and campaigns, all as one package. Rather than asking sellers to stitch it together manually, let the artificial intelligence do the work.

- Marketing should leverage their own channels in parallel to provide highly surgical air cover, using the same AI driven auto-personalization tactics, so that every customer still receives their very own tailored message that is highly consistent with sales communication.

- Sales needs to adopt modern practices with which to target prospects and customers using marketing data and auto-personalized messaging and content. Rather than going randomly after prospects and customers in their book of business, they should trust the data and work with marketing's campaigns.

Featured Technology:
Sales Enablement and Content Management

Folloze provides a customer engagement platform that empowers B2B enterprises to engage, develop, and win their target accounts by easily creating highly engaging and data-powered personalized experiences across every customer touchpoint. Built for scale and powered by its integrated experience, personalization, and orchestration engines, Folloze empowers marketing and sales teams to deliver jointly targeted and automated go-to-market programs to increase pipeline, close deals, and expand revenue with existing customers.

The Folloze customer engagement platform drives hyper-personalization via the following capabilities:

- **Real time hyper-personalization** of customer experiences including messaging, content, creative elements, and engagement actions

- **Personalization rules tool** that allows mapping of experience elements to any account or contact attribute

- **Dynamic seller mapping** that assigns account managers and account owners to their accounts' campaigns, and delivers comprehensive account engagement analytics

- **Field campaigns hyper-personalization** that applies personalization capabilities to any field-driven campaigns, initiated by either marketing or sales

- **AI and data aggregation** from a variety of platforms to build and act upon the richest and most up-to-date account and contact data and insights

These capabilities let organizations deliver hyper-personalized experiences designed by any marketer in the company and across all customer touch points, both for inbound and outbound strategies.

Cisco (http://bit.ly/folloze-cisco), for example, recently presented their highly orchestrated ABM engagement model, powered by Folloze, at the B2BMX conference. Their results were enlightening. Folloze let them build a comprehensive ABM program to deliver a data-driven, full-cycle, nine-figure pipeline.

Cisco integrated Folloze into their marketing stack to execute a fully end-to-end engagement strategy that unites account targeting, contextual sales enablement, sales outreach, customer content experience, and engagement analytics. The deployment was hugely successful and led them to conclude that Folloze was the only tool available that could integrate QlikView, SFDC, and Eloqua for customer engagement, providing visibility at each engagement point of the program.

Another Folloze customer, **Autodesk** described in a **press release (http://bit.ly/Folloze-AutoDeskCaseStudy)** how they were able to grow their ABM program from 0 to 10,000 accounts in one year. As a leader in 3D design, engineering, and entertainment software, engaging with their customers on a highly relevant and personalized basis was essential to their go-to-market strategy.

But they were challenged as to how to execute a personalization strategy that spans across marketing and sales and could scale to thousands of accounts. They concluded that Folloze uniquely let them address these challenges by delivering a simple-to-use, scalable personalization platform that allows marketing to equip sales with account-specific content for their customer communication, personalized by seller, industry, regions and customer role, empowering them to run a true marketing-powered sales motion.

As these organizations have seen, Folloze empowers an entirely new engagement model for marketing and sales teams. Folloze replaces the outdated model of marketing gathering leads and sending them over the fence to sales — which provides scale with no precision for Marketing, and precision but no scale for sales. Instead, Folloze creates an ABM motion and engagement model that yields extremely high consistency across the entire customer journey, at enormous scale and with unparalleled precision, and orchestrated by marketing and executed as a team with sales.

Sales Enablement and Content Management

AI For Sales Engagement has arrived, and companies like Folloze will continue to enable sales and marketing integration — powered by artificial intelligence — to change the game for sales and marketers.

The Vision - **One Integrated Journey**

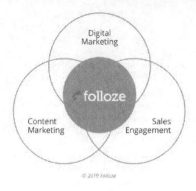

© 2019 Folloze

Chapter 8:

Outbound Prospecting / Agent-Assisted

As the former head of sales and marketing for a leading agent-assisted dialing company, I have a *soft spot* for sales technology that enables sales professionals to talk to their top prospects at will, as often as they want to.

And I also have *sore spot* from all the companies who get it wrong when deploying this technology. The biggest mistake—putting agent-assisted dialing in the hands of the wrong people, with the wrong messaging, and "accelerating suck" as Steve Richard, Founder and Chief Evangelist of ExecVision calls it!

I once saw a YouTube video of a monkey who was given a machine gun, you get the picture. Give agent-assisted dialing to an entry-level business development representative who hates rejection and hasn't yet learned how to talk to prospects effectively on the telephone and you might as well have handed a machine gun to a monkey!

As digital outreach becomes more and more crowded with all of the various vendor technologies, companies who invest in seasoned sales professionals to use agent-assisted dialing have a real competitive advantage versus those who hire entry-level sales professionals to do outbound prospecting.

Consider what a virtual assistant can do today:

- **Gather data** – Using tools like ZoomInfo Powered by DiscoverOrg and InsideView, a sales operations manager can automate data pulls so that the sales professional can focus on higher value work

- **Send highly personalized emails** – Now that the list has been pulled, AI can send (*and reply to*) email. It's not hard to map the right sentences to the right buyer personality and buyer type

- **Execute social outreach** – Technologies like FlowEngine.io and BDR.ai enable a sales professional to send highly personalized messages to people in their network asking for introductions to top target prospects

What's left for the sales professional to do?

ANSWER 1: If your job is to gather data, send personalized emails, and execute social outreach, probably not a whole lot unless you are really great at this function and could take the role on for an entire sales team (*otherwise known as Sales Operations*).

ANSWER 2: If your job is to sell solutions to companies, then the answer is simple, have more productive sales by automating the monotonous and labor-intensive work, have more productive conversations, and close 200% more than you could have closed before AI for sales.

Now that a virtual BDR can execute 300 – 500 digital sales activities (research, email, social) /day on behalf of the sales representative, sales representatives should be prepared to handle 2-3X more meetings than before the advent of AI for sales.

Technologies that will become a need-to-have versus a nice-to-have are scheduling technology, like Calendly and TimeTrade; proposal technology, like Qwilr; and conversation intelligence technology, like Chorus.ai.

For example, as CEO of ScaleX.ai, I personally run 8-12 sales conversations every day of the week (versus a typical sales person that might run 0-3 sales conversations per day). This requires me to ensure that my CRM is set-up in an optimal way, that presentations and proposals are easy to personalize and send with a few clicks, and that we have a super smooth customer onboarding process.

Featured Technology: Prospecting / Agent-Assisted

 scale^X.ai

ScaleX.ai One-Click Conversations™ provides the first ever fully integrated, agent-assisted dialing solution to an AI powered virtual assistant technology stack.

CHALLENGES ADDRESSED

- Close more deals with Always On Prospecting™ powered by virtual BDRs who execute up to 100 personalized emails and 100 social selling activities every day on client's behalf.
- Higher prospect engagement through outreach using personalized email, LinkedIn, and Twitter, and Agent-Assisted dialing.
- By providing five to ten times more sales activities, powered by artificial intelligence, clients see two to three times more meetings.
- Schedule more appointments with better data, personalization, social, and conversations to deliver the maximum number of meetings possible.
- More conversations from loading a list of cadenced or sequence call tasks, clicking "go," and talking to a prospect on the list in minutes.
- Better data quality and quantity working with data providers for valid emails and direct dial numbers.
- Improved adherence to sales process since BDR.ai follows your process.
- Improved skills by giving more time for sellers for learning and with improved coaching.
- Faster lead to response with marketing automation integration so leads are responded to immediately and called within minutes.

KEY PERFORMANCE INDICATORS

KPI 1: Fifteen to 50 meetings a month per seller.
KPI 2: Up to 1,000 leads per month matching the Ideal Customer Profile (ICP).
KPI 3: 100 personalized emails per day based on ICP.
KPI 4: 100 social activities per day including LinkedIn connection requests, InMails, Twitter likes, and more.
KPI 5: Eight to 10 conversations per hour with ICP-matched prospects.

KEY CAPABILITIES

✓ Append records with new and missing information from engagement with contacts and prospects.
✓ Determine ideal customer profile based on past engagement success.
✓ Set appointments for sellers.
✓ Determine emotional tone of interchanges.
✓ Automatically update CRM with relevant data.

Outbound Prospecting / Agent-Assisted

Within a few years, there will most likely not be any standalone agent-assisted dialing providers left—because they will have been gobbled up by CRM, sales engagement providers, or companies like ZoomInfo Powered by DiscoverOrg, who could at some point take on the whole space by merging multiple technologies into one whole solution.

The future of agent-assisted dialing … simply login to LinkedIn, tell your virtual bot that you'd like to dial all VPs of sales in Chicago and leave a message, and just like that, magic, a voicemail is recorded, the dialing starts, and 108 VPs of sales are called by the agent-assisted dialing platform. 78 voicemails were dropped and you had 4-5 conversations where you invited them to attend your event in Chicago next week. And it all happened in less than one hour.

The risk of agent-assisted dialing is that the B2B telephony and UCaaS providers are getting smarter about blocking robo-dialers. Over the summer of 2019, ScaleX.ai saw several customers go from a 35:1 dial-to-connect ratio to a 70:1 dial-to-connect ratio making it harder than ever to reach a prospect via the phone. We believe that companies in the agent-assisted dialing space will be required to leverage AI to swap caller ID's on the fly as telephony providers get smarter and smarter on call-blocking techniques.

Chapter 9:

Account and Opportunity Planning / Management

Account and opportunity planning / management is focused on helping companies win their most important deals, and to deploy an account-based selling strategy designed to map to a company's sales methodology and sales process.

Vendor Neutral has certified three companies in this space—infoteam.io, Membrain, and Prolifiq—each of whom integrate to Salesforce.com and one of whom offers a standalone CRM that is purpose built for account based selling—Membrain.

Key Capabilities of Account and Opportunity Planning/Management

CRM – accounts, contacts, pipeline; data enrichment; custom fields

Sales Enablement – sales process; content and templates; and training reinforcement

Sales Performance Management – goal management, trendline reporting, and team management

Productivity and Collaboration – integrated calendar and scheduler, integrated email inbox, shared email template

Featured Technology:
Account and Opportunity Planning / Management

MEMBRAIN

According to a report from Sales Benchmark Index, sales teams that follow a structured sales process achieve 48% higher win-rates.

Membrain makes it easy for sales teams to execute a sales strategy by actively guiding the sales team through a customer-defined sales process and playbooks.

Sales Analytics, powered by artificial intelligence

Real-time analytics that drive progress
With real-time access to the sales performance data that matters, you can focus on progress, not just activities. These insights power a data-driven approach that improves both forecast accuracy and win-rates.

Visual win/loss analysis

Use our win/loss analytics to understand why you win and lose. Detect your team's strengths and improvement areas. Improve forecast accuracy and win-rates by identifying the winning behaviors of top performers and quickly adjusting your entire team's workflow to follow.

Quickly identify improvement areas

Ensure that all team members understand their goals and receive the guidance to continually reach their targets with clearly defined key performance indicators. Get a visual representation of each team member's progress through the pipeline and break down quotas and objectives into actionable tasks. Capture the winning behaviors that lead to success and motivate your team by highlighting their progress and wins.

Customize powerful dashboards

Don't stop at "out of the box." Take our powerful analytics to the next level by dragging-and-dropping the most relevant sales information into your own easy-to-understand dashboard. Get the exact data you need, when you need it, delivered in a snapshot that works specifically for you.

Share beautiful presentations

Easily share regular progress reports with stakeholders by subscribing to beautiful, presentation-ready PDFs that provide an at-a-glance look at the health of your sales pipeline. Schedule these reports to be sent to any inbox, at regular times.

Customer Quote

"Membrain, out of the box, is the most complete sales enablement platform on the market. It has all of the right dashboards, analysis, behavior tracking, and process integration. And salespeople actually live in Membrain."

-Brian Kavicki, Lushin, Inc.

MEMBRAIN

CHALLENGES ADDRESSED

- Help sellers to learn and follow sales process and methodology using informative and actionable workflows.
- Improve and reinforce seller skills using guided selling, recommendations and integrated access to training content.
- Know who needs coaching and when based on analyzing actions and performance compared to goals.
- Better forecast deals using a milestone-based sales process.
- Iterate sales processes based on win/loss analytics.
- Reduce sales cycles by mapping strategy to actionable workflows.
- Quickly find the right content via a built-in content repository.
- Improve and reinforce seller skills using guided selling and recommendations and integrated access to training content.
- Shorten new hire ramp time by guiding sellers to best actions.
- Reduce number of tools/apps by embedding features in one solution.

KEY PERFORMANCE INDICATORS

- KPI 1: Increase win rates by using structured selling to guide sellers.
- KPI 2: Win bigger deals by workflows and coaching at every sales step.
- KPI 3: Improve quota attainment by following a sales process, tracking actions and alerting to coaching needs tied to goals.
- KPI 4: Reduce sales cycles by built-in scheduling and alerts of actions needed to support an opportunity.
- KPI 5: Faster new hire ramp-up since sellers are guided at every step.

KEY CAPABILITIES

- ✓ Know every detail about every opportunity, account, and lead from every system.
- ✓ Know which people from sales and customer sides are engaged, how senior they are and their relationships.
- ✓ Keep reps focused on the right process and priorities with automated, AI-driven "next best actions."
- ✓ Collaborate on opportunity activities and responsibilities.
- ✓ Identify referrals to help close deals.
- ✓ Keep close dates current with predictive update recommendations.
- ✓ Know which deals are in trouble (and why) before you miss a commit date.
- ✓ Track and monitor changes in deal status and the causes.

Account and Opportunity Planning / Management

Aligning sales processes within a CRM can be a daunting task. That's why these companies have created a multi-million dollar space to enhance this process, powered by AI to drive deep insights. In the 2018 B2B Buyers Survey DemandGen Report, 95% of buyers said that the sales reps demonstrating knowledge of their company and insights into their problems played an important role when evaluating solutions, with 64% considering if very important.

Thought leaders like Jamie Shanks, CEO of Sales for Life, and Gerhard Gschwandtner, CEO of SellingPower, predict a future where sales territories, and account-based selling, will be created by artificial intelligence. Whoever has "social proximity" as Jamie calls it, will work a specific account. Aligning the right personality with the right buyer personality is showing signs of an increase in sales. Watch for these tactics to be built into account and opportunity planning / management technologies in the future.

Chapter 10:

Video Selling

The Vendor Neutral Certified 100 Vendors in the video selling category are Videolicious and Consensus. Other established players in the space include Vidyard, BombBomb, and Co-Video.

With so much digital noise in today's selling environment, authenticity is more important than ever. This is why companies like Zoom Video have performed so well— bringing video to the selling motion enables sales professionals to be authentic and win more deals.

Having been a user of video selling for more than a decade, it's clear why this technology is gaining in popularity—it helps establish rapport (*and trust*) between the buyer and the seller.

From Video Selling Websites

- BombBomb's website – Rehumanizing your communication with BombBomb. Video email builds trust, converts leads, and wins referrals by getting you face to face more often.

- Vidyard's website – More than just video hosting. Generate and close more deals with the video platform trusted by the fastest growing companies.

- Covideo's website – Be seen. Be real. Begin. Your message heard, your personality on display, and your tool, Covideo. They're the video communication solution for businesses of all sizes.

- Consensus (**www.goconsensus.com**) – Scale your "standard demo" with interactive video demos.

- Videolicious – Engage better. Delight customers with professional quality, branded, personalized videos at scale.

- Rawshorts – Transform your articles and text into videos.

Featured Technology: Video Selling

Rawshorts is the only video selling solution that I've found that leverages artificial intelligence to create better videos— with very little effort and technical expertise required.

The user logs in, clicks on "Convert My Blog Post to Video", and the A.I. video creator builds a video explainer for the sender.

Video Selling

Rawshorts is a pioneer in leveraging AI for video selling. Imagine in just a few years from now, a sales professional will be able to create a video model of themselves—complete with mannerisms, eye movements, and more. What if the AI could look at a website or blog (like Rawshorts does today), create a powerful 60 – 90 second video explainer, and then add a video message from the sales rep—without the sales rep's involvement in its creation. Now couple that with JOYai enhanced messaging—what if the AI could create a one-to-one message based on the prospect's personality and buyer type. This isn't too far off.

Chapter 11:

Lead Engagement

Lead Engagement was created to provide AI for inbound lead engagement by the leader in the space, Conversica, over ten years ago. During that time, Conversica raised nearly $90M and has been uncontested – *until now*.

With the launch of the ScaleX.ai Virtual Assistant (*powered by Exceed.ai*), there are now two players in the market. When you combine the power of AI powered bots to automate email conversations and bring in a human to handle only the parts that require a human, you have ScaleX.ai.

Vendor Neutral has certified just two providers in this space — Conversica and ScaleX.ai.

The value of a virtual assistant

- **No lead slips through the cracks** - Engage every lead. Be certain you don't miss any revenue opportunity.

- **Timely engagement** - Reach out to leads fast, while they're still hot. Any lead volume. 24/7. Guaranteed.

- **Boost your funnel** - Qualify more leads, generate more meetings, and close more business deals faster with the power of our sales assistant.

- **As human as it gets** - Give prospects a seamless human experience, until they're qualified to speak to a real human agent.

Featured Technology: ScaleX.ai

ScaleX.ai was launched in July 2017 and in 2018 added solutions BDR.ai (a sales engagement platform focused on outbound business development) and SDR.ai (a sales engagement platform focused on lead nurture).

ScaleX.ai provides multi-channel sales acceleration as a service, powered by artificial intelligence.

What is multi-channel sales acceleration? Simply put, multi-channel sales acceleration leverages multiple channels of outreach to accelerate sales. These channels can include phone, email, social, and chat.

Example: A team of ten sales development representatives handling 2,000 inbound leads/month.

Before Lead Engagement Technology: Each sales development representative is routed 200 leads/month (10/day) and is responsible for making 3-4 dial attempts/lead, sending 4-5 emails over a 30-day period, and converting at least 20 leads/month into meetings.

The Inefficiency: Not all sales development representatives follow the prescribed process. Some make fewer dials, some email blast, some steps get skipped, and some SDRs are just better on a phone call than others.

The Investment (without lead engagement technology)

Sales Personnel and Technology	Annual Investment
1 Sales development manager	$170,000
10 Sales development reps	$750,000
10 Seats of prospect engagement technology	$12,000
10 Seats of manual dialer (125,000 dials/year)	$3,000
10 Seats of CRM	$15,000
Recruiting costs to replace 50% of the team each year	$100,000
Total annual cost of SDR team	$1,050,000
Lost sales due to lower conversion rates due to constant ramp-up (varies by product/segment)	-$250,000
TOTAL COST of people-centric SDR model	**$1,255,000**

The Investment (with lead engagement technology)

Sales Personnel and Technology	Annual Investment
1 Sales development manager	NA
2 sales development reps (1 phone, 1 digital)	$200,000
5 Virtual SDRs (lead engagement technology)	$30,000
1 Agent-assisted dialer (250,000 dials/year)	$100,000
2 Seats of CRM	$3,000
Recruiting costs to replace 50% of the team each year	NA
Total annual cost of SDR team	$333,000
Increase in sales due to higher performance of AI-powered Virtual Assistants	**+$250,000**
TOTAL COST of technology centric SDR model, powered by a few GREAT reps	**$63,000**

Whether the lost sales due to lower conversion rates are $25,000, $250,000 or $2.5M, this is the most important number of the equation when considering lead engagement technology. Most companies want to optimize for revenue first, and cost second, especially technology companies. Combining lead engagement technology (virtual SDRs) with highly competent human SDRs, who are equipped with agent-assisted dialing, will convert far more leads into opportunities. And, that will have a huge impact on pipelines and bookings.

Lead Engagement

As artificial intelligence becomes more and more prevalent to handle chat and email, the next logical channel is voice. Companies already leverage voice IVRs for inbound call center operations, why not for handling voice communications? Imagine AI-powered bots that can speak foreign languages and can map to the personality type of the caller. One of the speakers at the very first Alexa Voice Conference in 2018 said that if a bot could be programmed to handle communications, then adding a voice to the bot would be no problem.

Chapter 12:

eSignature

eSignature has been used by sales teams since the early 2000s and continues to facilitate commerce across all industries. As the technology matures—companies like DocuSign (who acquired SpringCM) and EchoSign (acquired by Adobe)—more complete solutions, powered by AI, will continue to evolve.

From their websites

- **DocuSign** - Save money, time and trees. Electronically sign, and now prepare, act on, and manage agreement to deliver great experiences for your customers and employees.

- **SpringCM** - A DocuSign company, helps generate, automate, manage, and store documents and contracts in our secure cloud. By simplifying business processes, companies can close business deals faster while making it easier for customers to work with a company because when documents flow, work flows.

- **Adobe Sign** – Let them sign on the digital line. Whatever your department needs signed, it's *swipe* and *tap* quickly with e-Signatures. Adobe Sign makes it level, secure, and digital—end to end.

The state of digital experiences among state governments has increased—governments today that adopt digital processes are finding greater efficiencies. For example, states that process 20,000 forms annually may save nearly $600k a year by going digital.

My first experience was with DocuSign at WebEx (pre-Cisco acquisition) in 2006. The value proposition: reduce sales cycle times by 20 – 30%, improve order accuracy, and ensure deals were booked for quarter-end. Prior to that, WebEx used paper faxes to book orders.

Featured Technology: DocuSign

Since its inception in 2003, DocuSign has been on a mission to accelerate business and simplify life for companies and people around the world.

DocuSign pioneered the development of e-signature technology, and today offer the world's #1 e-signature solution. It's just part of the broader cloud-based system of agreement platform, which allows companies of all sizes and across all industries to quickly modernize and digitize the entire agreement process—all the way from preparing agreements to signing, enacting, and managing them—from almost anywhere in the world, on practically any device.

DocuSign's value is simple to understand: legacy, paper-based agreement processes are manual, slow, expensive, and error-prone. DocuSign eliminates the paper, automates the process, and connects it to all the other systems that businesses are already using.

The DocuSign platform has 350+ prebuilt integrations with popular business apps. In addition, our API enables embedding and connecting DocuSign with customers' websites, mobile apps, and custom workflows. All told, today this enables more than 400,000 customers and hundreds of millions of users to measure turnaround times in minutes rather than in days, substantially reduce costs, and largely eliminate errors.

Fast facts

- More than 400,000 paying customers and hundreds of millions of users worldwide

- Seven of the top ten global technology companies

- Eighteen of the top twenty global pharmaceutical companies

- Ten of the top fifteen global financial services companies

- A quote from Forrester Research says "the strongest brand and market share leader [DocuSign] is becoming a verb."

eSignature

What is the future of eSignature? Consider what CLEAR has done for air travel. When you use CLEAR at the airport, your fingerprint is stored in the cloud, along with your retinal scan, and a ton of information. Might eSignature incorporate fingerprint scans and retinal scans? You bet.

Chapter 13:

Sales Assessments

Lori Richardson
CEO, Score More Sales @scoremoresales

Personality profiles such as DISC have been around since the 1940s and, in sales, are often used to hire, onboard, and align training for sales professionals. A lot has changed since the 1940s!

With the advent of big data and artificial intelligence, companies like Score More Sales' power clients work with two sales tools created by Objective Management Group (OMG) to ensure that companies hire the right sales professionals that both "can sell" and "will sell" and have the right reps and leaders in their existing sales team.

While you can talk with more than 100 other OMG partners, Score More Sales has created a process and infrastructure to help create successful outcomes every time, when you put a

Sales Candidate Assessment or a Sales Effectiveness Improvement Analysis (SEIA) in place in your company.

Score More Sales, powered by AI, focuses on measuring 21 core sales competencies plus underlying issues dubbed "sales DNA."

From the article "The Wrong Salespeople are Hired 77% of the Time," by Dave Kurlan, CEO, Objective Management Group, 94% of sales managers are optimistic about their salespeople. That's a very surprising statistic for a couple of reasons:

1. 50% or more of their salespeople won't hit their quotas this year and haven't since at least 2008.

2. Objective Management Group's (OMG's) findings from the evaluations and assessments of 1,882,486 salespeople show that 50% of all salespeople are weak.

Sales managers believe that 50% of their salespeople are good and 44% of their salespeople have potential. Of course, they are using subjective, rather than objective, approaches to measuring what "good" is.

How do you measure good?

- Salespeople consistently meet or exceed quota or expectations

- You like your salespeople, they work hard, don't give you any trouble, are positive, don't miss quota by too much, sometimes bring in good customers, are advocates of the company and brand, are good influences, etc.

Unfortunately, a lot of sales managers choose the second option.

Why? Many sales managers aren't very good at what they do! Only 10% of all sales managers are effective at both coaching and coaching consistently, and, when it comes to holding salespeople accountable, they aren't much better. Review the table below:

Competency	All Salespeople	Weak	Elite	Difference
Make Excuses	60%	67%	19%	352%
Lack Commitment	37%	53%	3%	1766%
Lack Motivation	20%	30%	0%	2000%
Lack Minimum Required Sales DNA	67%	97%	2%	4850%

- 60% of all salespeople make excuses for their lack of performance
- 37% of all salespeople lack commitment for sales success
- 20% of all salespeople are not motivated to achieve sales success
- 67% of all salespeople lack the minimum required "Sales DNA" for success in their roles

It's no wonder that sales managers are ineffective. While there is clearly work to be done in the area of coaching, the real problem is that they begin with the wrong salespeople!

Competency	All Sales Managers	Weak	Elite	Difference
Make Excuses	54%	68%	16%	425%
Lack Commitment	22%	35%	3%	1166%
Lack Motivation	45%	64%	12%	533%
Lack Minimum Sales DNA	56%	89%	<1%	8900%

Between sales management and HR, the wrong salespeople are selected as often as 77% of the time! And then we wonder why their salespeople don't hit quota, why sales managers can't coach them up, and why sales managers aren't quicker to terminate and replace underperforming salespeople (there's a fantastic chance that they'll replace them with someone even worse).

The first set of numbers above are for all salespeople. When we focus on the bottom 50% — the ones that don't hit quota, the ones who make up the majority in all sales organizations — it looks even worse:

- 67% of weak salespeople make excuses

- 53% of weak salespeople lack commitment for sales success

- 30% of weak salespeople are not motivated to achieve sales success

- 97% of weak salespeople lack the minimum required "Sales DNA" for success in their roles

Obviously, the biggest difference between all salespeople and the bottom 50% is their "Sales DNA." And the difference between weak and the elite top 5% is 4,850%! That's why, when good and bad salespeople interview for sales positions, they appear to be essentially the same. Their "Sales DNA," or lack thereof, rarely surfaces unless you know which questions to ask and how to ask them. So, if you're wondering whether you can be fooled when interviewing salespeople, the data would suggest that if half of all salespeople are weak, and 97% of that group have inadequate "Sales DNA," then you are being fooled at least half the time.

There are also two huge gaps — one that shows the elite top 5% are highly motivated 2,000% more often and have strong commitment 1,766% more often than their weak counterparts.

That's the primary reason why more and more companies have turned to assessments. According to CSO Insights' 2018 Sales Talent Study, companies that use assessments have 61% quota attainment and 14.6% attrition, versus 49% quota attainment and 19.8% attrition for those who don't use assessments. Companies that use assessments are 25% more successful at quota achievement and that data is not even for any particular assessment. Imagine how much better the results are for the companies that use OMG's predictive sales-specific candidate assessments. **Data from companies who have hired salespeople that were recommended by Score More Sales/OMG shows an attrition rate of only 8% and quota attainment of 88%.**

If you use OMG's sales-specific candidate assessments to filter and select your salespeople, you are less likely to make a hiring mistake than if you use an assessment that lacks predictive capabilities, and far less likely to make a mistake than if you don't use any assessment.

Assessments are mainstream — there are hundreds of them — and companies that ignore them are knowingly adding unnecessary risk and stunted growth to their revenue streams. According to Forbes, the cost of a bad hire is $240,000. But that's not for a sales hiring mistake — that's a generic hiring mistake. Factor in lost opportunities, lost customers, and lost revenue and that number can quickly and easily exceed $1 million per salesperson!

Why wouldn't you invest a tiny fraction of that to avoid costly mistakes? It's not like there's any risk. Take OMG for instance. As you can see from the screenshot below, it's been used on more than 1.8 million salespeople to hire more than 76,000 salespeople in more than 26,000 companies in 200 industries from 43 countries since 1990.

As for the accurate and predictive part, consider that of the candidates who are not recommended by OMG, but get hired anyway because the company is either desperate or stubborn, 75% fail within 6 months. And, of the candidates who are recommended and eventually hired, 92% rise to the top half of their sales organizations within 12 months. It is very accurate and predictive.

For more insight about your specific team, try Score MoreSales:

- **Free Sales Process Grader**
- **Free Sales Force Grader**
- **Free Hiring Mistake Calculator**

Do you want to know more about the Pre-hire, Sales Candidate Assessment or an analysis of your existing sales team from the standpoint of the reps, leaders, pipeline, and process? **Reach out here**.

Contact me **directly** (**https://www.scoremoresales.com/contact-us**) to talk further about your team's scenario at **lori@scoremoresales.com**.

Featured Technology: Sales Assessments

Score More Sales provides effective strategies to increase revenues through sales force development. These solutions include sales team evaluation; training; and coaching, and process improvement. Score More Sales is a top certified partner of Objective Management Group.

CHALLENGES ADDRESSED

* Identify who needs coaching and when.
* More accurate forecasts by identifying right skills needed by sellers.
* Reduce ramp time by hiring better candidates.
* Increase number of deals by targeting sellers with needed skills and aptitudes.
* Improve outcomes from each interaction between sellers and buyers.
* More appointments by hiring the right candidates.
* Increase prospect engagement and conversations.
* Improve quality of coaching for sales managers.
* Better adherence to sales processes.
* Increased win rates.

KEY PERFORMANCE INDICATORS

KPI 1: Stronger sales pipeline.
KPI 2: Faster onboarding and shorter ramp time.
KPI 3: Higher win rates.
KPI 4: Lower turnover.
KPI 5: Improved hiring Return-On-Investment (ROI).

KEY CAPABILITIES

✓ Assess knowledge and skills of candidates and current sellers.
✓ Faster onboarding by identifying skills based on assessments.
✓ Target high-value/potential candidates faster.
✓ Consistently assess sales candidates.
✓ Reduce time required to identify and assess candidates.
✓ Build objective evaluations of current employees and organization.
✓ Target and customize candidate assessments based on unique organizational requirements.
✓ Build assessments and tests for multiple sales roles.
✓ Deliver tests and assessments from any device.
✓ Compare and analyze results from any number of individual assessments.

Sales Assessments

If IBM can predict within 95% accuracy who is planning to leave their company by using artificial intelligence to make these predictions, you can bet that sales assessments are getting a facelift (powered by AI) too.

Everything at OMG is based on science and data. ScoreMoreSales / OMG has assessed or evaluated nearly 1.9M sales roles and the data tells quite a story.

- There is an elite 6%, another 20% who are good, and 74% who are weak and ineffective.

- 18% of all sales managers should not be in sales management.

- 34% of sales managers aren't trainable.

- Only 7% of all sales managers are effective at sales coaching.

- When companies hire sales candidates that we don't recommend, 75% of those salespeople fail inside of 6 months.

- When companies hire sales candidates we do recommend, 92% end up in the top half of their sales force within 12 months.

From OMG's website:

As artificial intelligence is leveraged in sales assessments, imagine the impact of getting the right reps aligned to the right roles, the right companies, and the right managers.

Chapter 14:

Mobile Selling and Content Engagement

Mobile selling and content engagement are essential for today's modern field sales professional. Empowering sales with the latest content in a simple-to-find and a simple-to-send approach, via a mobile device, is showing a real impact and sales ability to build more pipeline and close deals faster.

The value of these technologies

- Keeps your message consistent

- Shares the right content in seconds

- Keeps track of team activities

From their websites

MobileLocker – Effortlessly manage, share, and distribute your marketing materials and sales aids—all in one easy-to-use app!

Flipdeck – The right content makes you look good. Customers expect content that is targeted to them and up to date. Does it take too much time to assemble information to send to customers? How about when you're mobile? A Flipdeck account puts everyone on the same page with accurate, simple-to-locate content cards that you can mix and match to advance the sale. Give yourself an edge and make your business look good.

"I like how all the information I want to share is in one place – no hunting and pecking around." Cyndee Whipple, Ricoh USA

Featured Technology:
Mobile Selling and Content Engagement

Locate and share content

With Flipdeck, your frequently shared information is at your fingertips – so you don't have to go searching for the same links, docs, and videos every time you're asked.

Organize content into cards and decks

Flipdeck is designed around the idea of trading card decks – which have a visually consistent structure that makes it easy to quickly find a card at a glance.

Use Flipdeck to send just the right link

With a Flipdeck account, you can create cards for any content you want to share in our easy-to-use web application.

Here are some ideas of what you can share with your customers using your Flipdeck account.

- Product sec page
- Video
- Price sheet
- Brochure
- Testimonials
- Company profile
- Credit application
- Promotions

CHALLENGES ADDRESSED

- Find the right content to share and rapid creation of linked-content.
- Who needs coaching and when based on seller usage of content.
- Reduce sales cycles by matching the right content to the opportunity at every stage.
- Shorten new hire ramp time by sharing targeted content.
- Increase buyer engagement responding with content faster.
- Improve interaction outcomes by presenting content "on the fly" with buyers.
- Increase the number of buyer conversations by sending bite-sized content before meetings.
- Improve adherence to sales process or methodology using content designed for the process.
- Improve seller skills with teams collaborating and sharing content.
- Reduce the number of content platforms via a single portal to find and use content.
- Faster lead response by quickly creating and sharing content.
- Reduce the number of platforms in use with one tool to use to share content.
- Increase win rates with faster sharing of content with buyers.

KEY PERFORMANCE INDICATORS

- KPI 1: Reduce time sellers spend creating and finding content.
- KPI 2: Faster launches of new products by ensuring the right, easily consumable content is available and tracking how users share.
- KPI 3: Increase win rates with content that has been proven to work in the past.
- KPI 4: Improved brand consistency and compliance with the use of approved content.

Mobile Selling and Content Engagement

How will artificial intelligence impact mobile selling and content engagement? ANSWER: AI and machine learning can track all prospect and customer interaction and correlate the right content leads to the right actions. In the near future, like Netflix, content will be able to be configured by unique buyer personality and buyer type (think **JOYai**), to match the right messaging to the right buyer personality, based on how they communicate.

Chapter 15:

Sales Compensation

There is only one Vendor Neutral Certified 100 company in the sales compensation space—and that's Xactly Corporation. Other players include CallidusCloud, Oracle HCM Cloud, Oracle NetSuite, Oracle Incent, and IBM SPM. Some of the newer technologies include QCommission, Performio, Spiff, Iconixx Sales, Commissionly, CaptivateIQ, and Sales Cookie.

Sales compensation software automates the accounting and administration of commissions and incentive plans based on several customizable rules such as employee role, tenure, or sale type. In addition, it allows salespeople to view their quotas and progress while enabling management to generate reports to gain high-level insights into sales performance.

Sales compensation software is used by sales, accounting, and administration teams. Because sales compensation structures often differ from those of the rest of a business, these tools are purpose built for sales. This software is usually implemented as part of a broader compensation software infrastructure including payroll, accounting, or billing software. Many sales compensation tools also integrate with other sales tools, such as sales performance management, sales analytics, or sales gamification.

Featured Technology:
Mobile Selling and Content Engagement

Xactly Corporation is a leading provider of enterprise-class, cloud-based, incentive compensation solutions for employee and sales performance management. The company's flagship product, Xactly Incent™, gives enterprise companies robust features and capabilities to successfully design, implement, and manage their compensation programs.

With powerful functionality and an extensive module suite, Xactly Incent lets organizations increase ROI with optimized plans, improved efficiencies, and greater accuracy. Xactly Incent's intelligent automation lets organizations apply best practices to incentive compensation plans, while speeding routine processes to save time, reduce errors, and lower shadow accounting.

With a powerful calculations engine, Xactly Incent manages the most complex formulas with flexibility and ease. Xactly

Incent increases system efficiencies with the integration of compensation data with existing ERP, CRM, or HCM solutions. Xactly Incent provides fully native Android and iOS support, giving reps instant access to their commission results from any mobile device. Managers can easily view individual and team performance quota — anytime, anywhere.

Sales Compensation

In an SAP blog post, *7 Ways AI Helps Your Commission Plans In 2019*, you'll see the future of AI for sales compensation.

1. **Take the guesswork out of plan optimization.** Augmented intelligence eliminates guesswork with granular prescriptive compensation plan recommendations.

2. **Get optimal quota insight.** Understand if your sales team quota is too low, or too high. Are they incentivized to sell the right solutions?

3. **Get help assigning territories for optimal performance.** Do you know whether you've divvied up territories evenly and optimally?

4. Build trust with sales reps.

5. Maximize profits. Are you spending too much or too little on commission?

6. **Save time.** AI-enabled comp tools empower managers to introduce new commission plans in days, not months.

7. **Reduce consultant and professional fees.** Instead of creating comp plans internally, many organizations rely on consultants and professional services firms to draft plans for them—usually at a steep price. AI-powered commissions software enables companies to quickly and easily devise accurate comp plans with no outside experience required.

AI may seem like the stuff of the future, but it's already reshaping the way we live and do business.

"AI reduces the cognitive workload for sales operations and makes it possible to share actionable insight across all levels of the organization," SiriusDecisions said in a 2019 sales operations forecast.

By investing in an AI-enabled commission solution, your company can increase its agility and efficiency while building a team of motivated salespeople who strive every day to reach their full potential.

Chapter 16:

Knowledge Sharing

Knowledge sharing involves identifying, capturing, evaluating, retrieving, and sharing information assets. Assets managed by knowledge sharing software include documents, images, audio and video files, and other types of information. Knowledge sharing is the process of capturing, distributing, and effectively using knowledge, and making an organization's data and information available to the members of the organization and its partners and customers. Leading providers include Confluence, Stack Overflow, Guru, and Enablix.

The Vendor Neutral Certified 100 solo provider in this category is KIITE. AI-enriched sales playbooks, or "playbooks you'll actually use" are designed to give a sales team the best knowledge, at the right moments, without all the digging. And one of KIITEs's advisors is one of the sales greats of our time, Cory Bray, Managing Director of ClozeLoop. Cory's latest book, *Sales Playbooks: The Builder's Toolkit*, is featured in the KIITE AI-enriched sales playbook application. (If you ever meet Cory, ask him about the novel that he plans to write called *Dirt*.)

In a recent Sales 3.0 Conference, Joseph Fung, the CEO of KIITE shared the five keys to successful AI-enriched sales playbooks:

1. Design for search

2. Know your winning zone

3. Write for real-time use

4. There MUST be more than one

5. BOLO for hidden personal plays

Watch the full video here:
https://embed.vidyard.com/share/fypXWPMdnnBzPQk4oq QXLQ?

Another Knowledge Management Provider: Guru

Guru is a knowledge network that unifies your organization's collective knowledge, verifies its accuracy, and empowers your teams by bringing them the knowledge they need to do their jobs. Guru's AI Suggest contextually surfaces knowledge in the web browser, improving over time around user patterns and an organization patterns, making every piece of knowledge served across Guru's network more relevant and useful every day.

Today, Guru serves hundreds of leading modern enterprises such as Shopify, Square, Spotify, Autodesk, and Yext. By bringing your team the knowledge they need in all of the applications they use, you can expect to see the following outcomes using Guru:

- Increased adoption and trust of knowledge

- Decrease in employee onboarding time

- Decrease in time to first response

- Decrease in handle time

- Increased competitive win rates

- Decreased sales cycles

- More valuable conversations with customers that drive revenue

Featured Technology: Knowledge Sharing

A well-designed, relevant, and highly utilized sales playbook creates teams that engage with more prospects, produce more pipeline, and close more deals.

A playbook creates more consistent top performers more quickly. It will also close the gap between your top performers and everyone else.

Unfortunately, 95% of playbooks are dead upon arrival because of

- Poor development process

- The wrong content

- Static delivery and no engagement

Building a sales playbook isn't hard; building an effective sales playbook which contributes to revenue is.

Kiite's AI-powered assistant helps sales teams increase productivity and competence by providing real-time coaching and answers to questions within existing chat systems such as Slack. Kiite surfaces the information sales reps need when they need it, and proactively provides leadership with insights into knowledge gaps.

CHALLENGES ADDRESSED

- Access situational and subject matter experts.
- Know who needs coaching and when by tracking who is asking and what questions.
- Shorten sales cycles with answers to questions at moment of need.
- Reduce ramp time by answering questions using A.I.
- Better outcomes from each interaction since sellers can get answers to prospect questions faster.
- Improved coaching quality based on analysis of question patterns.
- Better use of sales processes and methodologies.
- Increase win rates by having the right information at the right time.
- Use fewer platforms and tools via better collaboration.

KEY PERFORMANCE INDICATORS

KPI 1: Increase selling time by reducing time spent searching for answers.

KPI 2: Increase efficiency and scaling of subject matter expertise.

KPI 3: Increase visibility into knowledge gaps and training opportunities.

KPI 4: Reduce sales cycles by providing reps with the microcontent they need to facilitate customer conversations.

KPI 5: Fewer compliance issues by surfacing only accurate and approved answers.

KEY CAPABILITIES

- ✓ Automatically recommend content based on questions.
- ✓ Capture and analyze recommendations to inform future strategy.
- ✓ Develop insights based on seller questions to better engage prospects.
- ✓ Just-in-time training integrated into workflow tied to the sales cycle.
- ✓ Plan account-specific strategies based on analysis of questions related to opportunities.
- ✓ Pull data from sources such as the CRM and present data in real-time.
- ✓ Share, access, and collaborate using a common knowledge base.
- ✓ Understand prospects' business needs and challenges.

Knowledge Sharing

Tools like Guru are leading the way in AI for sales in knowledge sharing. AI Suggest contextually surfaces knowledge in the web browser, improving over time, around user patterns and organization patterns, making every piece of knowledge served across Guru's network more relevant and useful every day. In other words, these AI systems get smarter over time—just like you have read about and seen in the movies!

Chapter 17:

Conversation Intelligence

Conversation intelligence has been around for several years and was first used by large call centers to track, monitor, and optimize inbound calls. The software would convert conversations into text, and capture information such as length of call, tonality of the call, and other things.

Conversation intelligence (CI) software is a machine learning-infused sales training software tool that helps sales organizations optimize and improve their ability to close deals. CI software records sales calls and facilitates playback, transcriptions, and scoring, so that both sales representatives and sales managers can identify highs and lows. With CI software, sales orgs can leverage and disseminate best practices to all reps, as well as unlock hidden insights that exist in the current CRM. Ultimately, CI software's coaching and development functionalities encourage knowledge sharing, improve sales processes, and optimize pipelines.

"If you have a team of 100 – or 1,000 – sales people, they can be in customer meetings, all day, every day, having the most important interactions with your customers," says Roy Raanani, CEO and Co-Founder of Conversation Intelligence Platform, **Chorus.ai (https://www.chorus.ai)**. "As an organization, you have no visibility or understanding into what's being discussed. Whether or not the sales people are on message, delivering the right points, handling situations the right way, as well as capturing the learning that you share back from the market. And that is essentially the problem that we set out to solve.

"You go from essentially being blind to all of these conversations, to having real visibility and understanding into what's happening. And once Go-To-Market teams have that visibility, and that understanding, they can do some really powerful things. For the first time ever, you can start to see the patterns in what your most successful employees are doing and spread those behaviors across the team."

Featured Technology: Conversation Intelligence

Overview: Chorus.ai is a Conversation Intelligence Platform that records, transcribes, and analyzes business conversations in real-time to coach reps on how to become top performers. With Chorus.ai more reps meet quota, you ramp new hires faster, coach the existing team effectively, and everyone in the organization can collaborate over the actual voice of the customer.

Enhanced visibility into a sales team's most critical asset

Only 5% of information on customer facing calls ever make it into the CRM. Chorus.ai is the first platform built to capture all customer facing conversations to seamlessly search, share, and analyze these critical moments.

AI powered insights to increase team productivity

Chorus's proprietary algorithms are trained on the collective learnings of the top B2B revenue teams, as well as a sales team's own best practices to help shorten ramp times, increase close rates, and coach reps at scale.

Surfacing moments and deals that impact revenue

Chorus's advanced AI also layers in insights to make sense of the huge volumes of conversation data to ensure maximum outcome advantage for the customer. It proactively surfaces important coaching moments and deals at risk, so if managers only have an hour to spend, they automatically know which deals or calls to listen to.

Customers Include: Zoom, TrustRadius, Qualtrics, AdRoll, Adobe, Marketo, ZoomInfo Powered by DiscoverOrg, ProCore, Outreach and GitLab.

CH〰RUS

CHALLENGES ADDRESSED

- Know who needs coaching with deal views, check how sellers are following the sales process, and search for any talk track.
- More accurate deal forecast by checking if sellers are using the right messaging and how they are following the sales process.
- Shorten sales cycles and increased win rates by surfacing critical deals based on risk factors and next steps.
- Faster ramp times with sellers listening to successful conversations and with practice and review of role-play conversations.
- Better outcomes from each interaction by analyzing how well sellers are following successful talk tracks.
- Improve quality of coaching by tracking how much time managers are spending coaching and using real conversations for review and training.
- Better process adherence by tracking seller behavior at every stage.
- Improve seller skills by targeting training and coaching based on actual conversations.
- Increase seller productivity by automatically surfacing next steps or calls to review and updating CRM deal data with meeting history and notes.

KEY PERFORMANCE INDICATORS

KPI 1: Shorter ramp time.
KPI 2: Increase in win rates.
KPI 3: Higher quota achievement.
KPI 4: Better competitive win rates.
KPI 5: Reduced sales cycle times.

KEY CAPABILITIES

- ✓ Analyze recorded sales calls for increasing win rates and improving coaching opportunities.
- ✓ Transcribe calls in text form in real-time and summarized based on conversation themes.
- ✓ Identify usage or frequency of keywords and phrases and their impact on win rates with Mention Analytics.
- ✓ Map seller speaking time vs. prospect speaking time.
- ✓ Share calls in a library with sellers with custom playlists based on call content.
- ✓ AI-curated playlists automatically surfaces important calls for sellers, managers, or leaders to review.
- ✓ Report on how well sellers adhere to scripts.
- ✓ Use call scores as a basis for lead qualification and next steps.
- ✓ Automatically update CRM with relevant call data with detailed notes on attendees, next steps, link to recording, and more.
- ✓ Provide coaching tips and alerts to sales managers.

Conversation Intelligence

Conversation intelligence continues to evolve. Imagine a new-hire joins your company and is able to listen to a dozen actual sales calls, complete with the coaching notes. How did the rep do discovery? How did they handle objections? Did they ask for a next step? Now imagine, the new rep starts to have sales calls with prospects. A manager can't always be on every sales call; however, the Chorus AI Assistant can. As sales methodologies are built into conversation intelligence platforms, in the near term, reps will get daily (and even real time) coaching from the AI-powered assistant.

Chapter 18:

Skills Development and Reinforcement

The Future of Learning: 17 Training Innovations that Lead the Way (Provided by the Sales Enablement experts at SPARXiQ)

Since the development of the World Wide Web in 1989, learning and development (L&D) professionals have needed to evolve with the onslaught of new technologies. There was a time when instructor-led classrooms with chalkboards were the only option for training. Presently, we see online courses and virtual training becoming the norm. But that's today-- what exciting advances do the future of learning hold?

In his book, *Landmarks of Tomorrow,* Peter Drucker coined the term **knowledge worker (https://en.wikipedia.org/wiki/Knowledge_worker).** Drucker defined knowledge workers as "high-level workers who apply theoretical and analytical knowledge, acquired through formal training, to develop products and services." Today, most successful organizations are teaming with knowledge workers and incorporate learning as a critical component of their strategic plans.

It's important to differentiate "learning" and "training." Training is a subset of learning and usually occurs when a new initiative has begun or for compliance purposes. It is not part of most employees' daily tasks. However, as training is an investment, learning gained during training needs to transfer to the workplace. With the advent of the knowledge worker, employees need to learn every day to be responsive to the fast pace of business. And employers need to ensure this learning aligns with organizational goals.

The purpose of this paper is to explore the seventeen innovations occurring to the methods of training and learning. Some are in their infancy; others are more mature. Additionally, we'll suggest some neuroscience-based practices to help you develop your organizational training.

1. Video

More than ever, training is offered via video. Why? Because videos both enhance traditional online learning, and they appeal to the learners of the YouTube generation. If you want to learn how to do something today, you can simply You Tube the topic and be offered a number of short videos to answer your questions. Companies are outsourcing formal learning content development to experts who develop **Hollywood-Style engaging videos (http://bit.ly/HollywoodStyleVideos)**. Once the videos are created, they are made available as formal learning experiences to be watched at an employee's desk, on their mobile devices, or at home on a laptop. They can be watched many times and revisited often. Another advantage to video is that they are easier to produce and put online than traditional learning materials.

According to **Forrester Research (http://bit.ly/forrester-75percent)**, "people are 75% more likely to watch videos than to read print." Other experts have concluded that after three days we tend to remember 10% of the information we saw in Word format, whereas we tend to retain 65% of the information we see in picture and Word formats **(http://bit.ly/picture-effect)**.

It's no mystery why videos have become the quick go-to method for learning something outside of work, from fixing your water heater to learning healthy ways to eat, and they are a staple in our everyday lives. Thus, many organizations are leveraging YouTube and Vimeo as their learning platforms. Not surprisingly **Statista.com (http://bit.ly/statista-video)** observes that there are about 192 million YouTube viewers in the U.S. alone, which is why learning and development professionals are tapping into that market. If you're not using videos … start now.

Ultimately, the goal is that your learning content becomes binge-worthy (like Netflix) and not cringeworthy. Think about it, would you prefer to stream a TV series or watch a narrated PowerPoint?

2. Mobile Training

Yes! Experts have been lauding **mobile training (http://bit.ly/LI-mobilelearning)** for many years now, so, somewhat annoyingly, so why hasn't it happened yet? Because—while necessary—many companies don't have the resources to implement the initiative. In the next two to five years, mobile training will rise to the top of essential learning strategies; once more, companies will make the leap to implement it.

According to **Restaurant Business Online,** more than half of all businesses have started using mobile learning, so it's an area ripe for growth. Mobile device users learn using their devices every day at their leisure. Someday mobile learning could be a part of their typical workday — providing just-in-time learning experiences that are repeatable to ensure retention.

3. Virtual Reality / Augmented Reality

Virtual and augmented reality is here! And, a small minority of companies are leveraging it. According to **CNBC (http://bit.ly/CNB-AugmentedReality),** UPS has seen its retention rate climb to 75% since they started using virtual reality in their training. More and less expensive, VR learning tools are being developed.

Also, virtual reality hardware is maturing and, correspondingly, the cost is decreasing. And the **research (https://www.td.org/insights/research-backs-benefits-of-vr-training),** oh the **research (https://techtyche.com/benefits-of-virtual-reality/)!** There is plenty of research conducted that proves the benefits of using virtual and augmented reality in training.

4. Flipped Classroom Experience

For years, many organizations have delivered learning programs using instructor-led designs. Unfortunately, many of these programs were designed to be easy for the instructor to deliver and not necessarily for the learner to retain. Hence, the traditional training format that entails hours of PowerPoint slides read by the presenter has been ridiculed and nicknamed "**death by PowerPoint (https://whatis.techtarget.com/definition/death-by-PowerPoint).**"

We know from the research on the **forgetting curve (https://en.wikipedia.org/wiki/Forgetting_curve)** this model is ineffective and that **most training (90%) is lost within 24 hours if not reinforced (https://en.wikipedia.org/wiki/Forgetting_curve).** Also, the longer the training is, timewise, the lower the ROI you'll achieve for your investment.

For now, some organizations will keep using instructor-led training; however, they will use a **flipped classroom design (https://www.sciencedirect.com/science/article/pii/S03601315 16301166).**

Here's how it works: first, knowledge transfer occurs before the training experience in a variety of modes (reading, videos, etc.), next, the training is then reinforced by participants by demonstrating their application of the knowledge. Often, the trainee will be training others in their cohort.

5. Personalized Learning

Personalized learning is now in its infancy. While there is plenty of scuttlebutt, organizations are having difficulty with implementation. In a study done by **RAND**, it was revealed when personalized learning was used on students that they achieved more significant academic progress than traditional students.

Employees each have their individual experiences that companies need to value and then build on by allowing a more personalized approach to learning. Leveraging pre-training assessments and deploying training based on skills gaps is one manner in which leading organizations are creating learning experiences that are both personalized and scalable.

For example, when it comes to sales training, once your team decides on the sales competencies, your sellers need sales skills assessments (today and in the future) that can be deployed to test for those competencies. If the trainee demonstrates a knowledge gap and a skills gap, training can be assigned, so that the trainee has a personalized learning experience. Best practice can also include managerial recommendations based on observations from the field. Fundamentally, assessments coupled with field observation enables personalized learning plans that drive the maximum performance improvement in minimal time.

6. Human-to-Human Skills Development

As a growing percentage of the workforce is comprised of born-digital millennials and generation Z, we've recognized a skills gap in human-to-human interaction abilities. Otherwise known as "soft skills," skills gaps have been identified for these generations in the areas of emotional intelligence and situational awareness.

Salespeople, in particular, must develop skills like understanding their personality style, recognizing the styles of others and adapting their style to sell to the other types. Increasingly, the need for **conversational intelligence (http://bit.ly/huffpost_ci)** and **commercial conversational**

development
(http://conversationaldevelopment.com/principles/) is expected to grow. Besides, research on this born-digital demographic shows a gap in traits like **empathy**, making eye contact, and presentation skills. Training in soft skills will be required to give their customers the best overall buying experience.

Author and sales enablement leader Anita Nielsen shares in her book, *Beat the Bots: How Your Humanity Can Future-Proof Your Tech Sales Career*, that human-to-human interaction skills will be the differentiation for most sales organizations.

7. Performance and Application

While developing learning objectives for training, we think "we need our learners to be able to do X at the end of this course" but often have a hard time figuring out the best way to ensure they are able to do X at the end of the training. The difficulty in proving the end result is why we will see performance driving more learning outcomes.

As **ATD** (**https://www.td.org/insights/the-future-of-learning-is-not-training**) puts it, "training will focus on performance, not smiles." Organizations want learners to take what they learned and use it to perform better on the job, teach another employee, or apply the learning outside of the classroom. Applied learning is the key to the future of learning.

At this point, there are several technologies that enable trainees to record application exercises in short videos that transform into application practice and can be shared in a peer-learning environment. Plus, managers are coached and encouraged to post coaching videos for each application exercise.

Allego (https://www.allego.com/), for example, has developed a platform that equips teams to maximize their learning experience with peer-to-peer learning.

8. Microlearning

If you are not practicing **microlearning (https://en.wikipedia.org/wiki/Microlearning)** in your training, you are already behind.

There is a lot of research backing **microlearning (https://www.businessnewsdaily.com/10504-microlearning.html)** and the positive effects it has on the learning process. Also, learners respond positively to microlearning because they can learn and still manage their time in a workday.

In practice, microlearning uses a chunking approach where topics are grouped into mini topics and taught one at a time. Importantly in microlearning, the pace is decided by the user. **Elearning Industry (https://elearningindustry.com/microlearning-macrolearning-research-tell-us)** notes that "good chunking shows the organization of the topic, which supports mental processes and helps people build usable knowledge." We live in a time where people need to learn and build on what they learn all the while being on the go. It's early days yet, but microlearning seems to address some of these challenges.

9. The Shift in Training Concentration

Historically, most sales training programs have been heavily weighted in favor of product features, benefits, and application training. Worryingly, some training programs have spent as much as 80% of the training time focused on product training and only 20% of the time spent on sales and soft skills development.

In the future, training programs will flip the time allocated to product training and sales skills training to make sellers skilled in sales skills, situational awareness, emotional intelligence, business acumen, entrepreneurial skills and how to connect and have a conversation with C-suite executives.

Training programs will have 80% of their curricula dedicated to developing skills to equip sellers to be **trusted advisors for their customers** **(http://www.nosmokeandmirrors.com/2018/07/13/achieve-sales-goals-turn-sales-reps-into-trusted-advisors/)**, providing valuable insights that have measurable economic outcomes for the customer.

Product training is important, but how it will be delivered and the amount of concentration of training time allocated will be reduced significantly.

10. Gamification

Is **Gamification** **(https://en.wikipedia.org/wiki/Gamification_of_learning)** just a buzzword? While we have all seen the articles, the demos, and heard the discussions, few companies have fully integrated it into their training.

According to the **Huffington Post** **(https://www.huffpost.com/entry/gamification_b_2516376?g uccounter=2)**, companies like Target were able to improve employee satisfaction while also reducing company costs by using Gamification. Target's employee demographic is perfect for Gamification, as it appeals to generations who grew up gaming and are still gamers during their leisure time. For most learners, part of Gamification's appeal is that when a user is challenged and a goal needs to be achieved, Gamification leverages the natural human reaction to fun. And the challenges can drive learner motivation, which can eventually provide a significant performance gain for your organization.

Salespeople, in particular, are very competitive by nature and gamification fuels this desire to compete and win.

11. Social Learning

We have seen interest in social learning—sometimes called informal learning or **peer-to-peer learning** (**https://www.tandfonline.com/doi/abs/10.1080/0144341050034 5172**)—starting to rise, and this will continue to become more common.

Social learning is where a learner learns something through non-traditional methods such as emails, conversations, social media, videos of peers completing application exercises, and discussion boards. **Topyx.com (https://www.topyx.com/lms-blog/research-shows-companies-encourage-social-learning**) states that social learning "accounts for at least 75% of the knowledge people attain in the workplace" usually unintentionally or not planned out.

Intentional social learning in organizations is immature and unintentional. Organizations are just starting to purchase platforms that will enable more structured social learning and develop strategies on how to manage social learning. **Topyx (https://www.topyx.com/lms-blog/research-shows-companies-encourage-social-learning)** also states that "companies that don't plan for informal learning will have no influence over at least 70 percent of the information their employees take in at work."

Today's learners have grown up using social learning in their everyday lives, so it's essential to incorporate it into corporate learning. However, organizations need a strategy and a plan to assimilate it.

12. Relevance - Pull vs. Push

We know the importance of making learning relevant; it provides more retention and engagement from the learner. But it is difficult to provide relevant learning when each learner has a different need.

Recently, L&D professionals have "flipped the script," and they are starting to look at training through the lens of how learners want to learn. For instance, when an employee is at home, they have immediate access to information when they need to learn something quickly.

Allowing staff learners to adopt a similar philosophy, it can be very beneficial for learners to pull the information they need when they need it (from an intranet or wiki), as opposed to having information pushed at them when and how you feel they need it.

In an article from **ATD** (**https://www.td.org/insights/the-future-of-learning-is-not-training**), the writer states that learners "will need to learn to **pull the information** (**https://www.linkedin.com/pulse/leverage-mobile-learning-enable-sales-skill-mark-allen-roberts/**) they need from a variety of resources rather than wait around for the information to be pushed to them."

Essentially, learning departments will need to have resources available and accessible when learners need them. We need to spend more time creating a database of instructional material (online courses, videos, documents, etc.) learners can work through on their own and are searchable by keyword.

13. Apps

We all have apps on our phone — gaming apps, workout apps, business apps, etc. But how can apps be used in training? According to **Elearning Industry,** some benefits to using mobile apps in training include easy accessibility on and offline, the delivery of just-in-time information, fostering higher completion rates, and ease-of-use for employees.

Some companies are venturing into building apps to onboard employees. A study by **Mindspace (http://bit.ly/mindspace-apps)** shows that onboarding a new employee can cost up to 22% of their annual salary; however, effective onboarding can help save time and costs. If conducted via an app, onboarding can become easily accessible, easily navigated, and familiar to employees, which means they are much more likely to take the time to work through the items in the app.

Elearning Industry states that apps are useful to offer "a series of microlearning nuggets," as well as to "push data that can help learners achieve mastery" and "provide on-the-job support." It might be time to start thinking about how your company could benefit from using apps for learning and onboarding in the future.

14. Remote Teams

Increasingly corporations are working with remote teams. In fact, **SkiptheDrive.com (https://www.skipthedrive.com/21-**

statistics-about-remote-work-trends-in-2018/) says, "remote working will rival fixed office locations by 2025" and "regular work-at-home, among the non-self-employed population, has grown 140% since 2005."

What does this mean for learning? We have to get better at training people who are not in the classroom. Virtual and eLearning are helping to accomplish this, but new technologies are emerging that will also enable a better learning experience for remote workers. For example, virtual training with video capabilities, or virtual training where the trainer can guide the learner through practice exercises are becoming more valuable.

These tools allow learners to feel like they are in a classroom because they can see each other, learn from each other, and still get one-on-one attention from the trainer. One of the hardest things to do in a virtual setting is to make learners feel like they are not alone, but new training methods and tools are enabling us to do just that.

15. Leveraging Assessments

In the future, sales trainees will not enter training programs without first taking a sales skills assessment. The new assessments will evaluate sales skills and competencies as well as the trainee's beliefs, social style, and motivations.

The results of these assessments will be used to design AI-powered personal learning plans for the trainee that are the material they want and need and delivered at just the right time. Assessments based on sales competencies can be delivered frequently to measure progress and identify opportunities for growth. Plus, the manager-observed behavior assessments could be integrated into monthly one-on-one coaching.

The future of assessment tools will not only share each salesperson's skill levels based on sales competencies, beliefs, and motivations but—in the world of big data—will also produce entire team reports, and these reports will be compared with other market-leading companies. Wow!

16. Holograms

Wait? What? Holograms? Like in the movies? Yep, that's right; holograms could become a learning tool in the future. In her book, *The Art and Science of Training*, Elaine Beich mentions one possibility that, in the future, the "classroom goes to the learner" and "interaction occurs in holographic rooms."

New technology like TeleHuman 2 mentioned in **New Atlas (https://newatlas.com/telehuman-2-hologram/54400/)** "enables real-time holograms of people to appear in any location." Can you imagine what it would be like to train a room full of holograms in real-time? So, why would holograms be beneficial in learning? Because they offer a live, more personalized experience, immersing the learner into the classroom from miles away. And because holograms are cool!

17. Employees Own Their Training

Just as buyers are now in charge of the buying process, salespeople will be in charge of their own training in the future. Today, depending on how your team is structured, sales training can report to human resources, sales, sales operations, marketing, sales enablement, and/or talent development. The leader of the training department meets with executives in sales and determines the sales competencies sellers must have and designs and delivers training. Some teams will have manager-observed skills assessments, and some training programs are designed to fill observed skills gaps. However, ultimately, it is the team itself who will determine training needs.

Once competencies are identified and assessments are completed, employees will design their own learning experience based on their needs and skills gaps. These learning plans will be monitored by their managers. The days of some poor soul in L&D monitoring and often prodding salespeople to complete courses are over. L&D will add much more value identifying skills gaps and producing learning experiences to close common skills gaps. L&D will own the learning assets with sales and the platform and overall learning experience.

The Future is Now

The future trainee will have personalized learning plans based on assessments and required skills with skills gaps already identified. Overarchingly, trainees will "own" their own training. The general manager of learning and development will analytically review training needs and develop courses to close skills gaps.

L&D leaders will monitor the course assessments and strategically add courses to close common skills gaps. The trainee will then be responsible for taking the classes and passing assessments and field application exercises to demonstrate they understand the skills required to do their job.

The goal is that learning is a continuous process. In particular, salespeople will have new learning plans each year. As they manage and complete their training, they will improve their value to the organization and give their customers the best experience possible.

As new technologies and methodologies become mainstream, L&D professionals and business leaders need to evolve continually. It's an exciting time for learning leaders as traditional classrooms and static eLearning, transform to a more connected and engaging online experience using a variety of methods and tools with a more personalized, relevant approach.

Finally, more and more sales teams realize that it's not *what* they sell but *how* they sell and serve their customers that becomes their distinctive competence and differentiator.

References

Biech, E. (2017). The Art and Science of Training. Alexandria, VA: ATD Press.

CMI. 20 Ways to Save Money on Your Next Video [ebook]. Retrieved from
http://comprehensivemedia.com/wp-content/uploads/Comprehensive_Media_20_Ways_To_Save_eBook02.pdf

Employee Onboarding + Training [blog post]. Retrieved from
https://www.mindspace.net/employee-onboarding-and-training?gclid=CjwKCAjw0ZfoBRB4EiwASUMdYQjoYMdJ DbnIasImYSCUyV9MUFMedequ0j0Dft3mO4YSOPPy5aFJN RoChWYQAvD_BwE

Gill, S., Grebow, D. (2017, February 10). The Future of Learning is not Training [blog post]. Retrieved from https://www.td.org/insights/the-future-of-learning-is-not-training

Hernandez, B. (2018, September 7). Statistics About Remote Work Trends in 2018 [blog post]. Retrieved from https://www.skipthedrive.com/21-statistics-about-remote-work-trends-in-2018/

Morris, C. (2018, October 30). Why Walmart and other F500 Companies are Using Virtual Reality to Train the Next Generation of American Workers [blog post]. Retrieved from https://www.cnbc.com/2018/10/29/why-f500-companies-use-virtual-reality-to-train-workers-of-the-future.html

Nield, D. (2018, April 27). Life-Sized 3D Holograms Could Be Coming to Your Next Videoconference [blog post]. Retrieved from https://newatlas.com/telehuman-2-hologram/54400/

Pandey, A. (2018, January 2). 4 Killer Examples of Using Mobile Apps in Corporate Training [blog post]. Retrieved from https://elearningindustry.com/mobile-apps-in-corporate-training-4-killer-examples-using

RAND Corporation, Bill and Melinda Gates Foundation (2015). Continued Progress: Promising Evidence on Personalized Learning.

Featured Technology:
Skills Development and Reinforcement

SPARXiQ provides modern, impactful, and memorable sales training that delivers true skills mastery to drive long-term profitability and growth. Customers include Cardinal Health, Dexter, Graybar, Orbit, and more.

As the technology and the buyer's journey have evolved, so has the role of the salesperson. Customers no longer look to sellers for low-level needs like order entry and product information. That means it's more critical than ever to strengthen sellers' core skills so that they create value in every customer interaction and build long-term, transformational relationships. Deep learning isn't just for machines — it's for people too.

If you want to change business outcomes, you must change daily behavior. Featuring interactive case studies, role playing and exercises, SPARXeQ is designed to engage the busy seller, who can learn the memorable content on the go. Our four tracks (quotients) are focused on critical skills that will help your team drive world-class profitability and exponential growth.

Skills Development and Reinforcement

IBM can predict with 95% accuracy when an employee is likely going to leave the company.

Link to the article: **http://bit.ly/IBM95Percent**

AI, which has replaced thirty percent of IBM's HR staff, can help employees identify new skills training, education, job promotions, and raises.

The future of skills development and reinforcement will be powered by artificial intelligence—what training to deliver, when to deliver it, how to deliver the training to optimize for performance, and the like.

Chapter 19:

Sales Training Content

When you Google *"sales training"* you'll find a handful of paid ads show up—including SalesBuzz, Janek, Brainshark, and Dale Carnegie Professional Sales Skills Training Program. When you visit G2 Crowd, you find their top two are JBarrows sales training and The Harris Consulting Group (led by Richard Harris, who has been voted a Top 25 Inside Sales Professional for the past five years in a row).

There are thousands of sales training books and methodologies available today, but not too many focus on inside sales methodologies, and not too many prescribe a "cadence" for sales coaching—Factor 8 does, and the Sales Bar has brought all relevant modules online for on-demand consumption by sales professionals.

In the Introduction of the book, *The Cadence of Excellence: Key Habits of Effective Sales Managers,* by Matthew McDarby, Matt highlights the problem with traditional sales coaching and the solution to the problem, which is broken down into two parts—inwardly focused and outwardly focused.

Introduction

The number one problem I hear from virtually every sales manager I interact with is, "I don't have enough time to do ALL the things that I need to do." As a result, some really important parts of their job are not done particularly well. Sales management can be a lonely and unforgiving job.

I realized roughly a decade ago while working as a client executive for one of the preeminent sales performance companies, Huthwaite (founded by noted behavioral researcher Neil Rackham), that the difference between being an excellent leader and being just average — or worse — depends largely on the choices one makes with his or her time. I realized that if someone were able to help sales managers make better choices with their time and effort, then that would have a huge impact on the performance of the whole sales organization.

I experienced this first-hand and learned invaluable lessons by observing great leaders in action. In 2010, I started United Sales Resources, and I have devoted the last seven years to helping sales managers — from frontline sales managers to chief sales officers —become dramatically more efficient and effective leaders.

The main premise behind my current business is that if you want to significantly improve the performance of your salesforce, focus on becoming a strong and effective sales manager by solving the "no time for important things" problem that I just described.

To be clear, this is not a book about time management. This is a book about the enormous impact your choices can have on your performance and on the performance of your entire team.

Consider for a moment the choices you make every day, month, or quarter about how you will apply your effort and focus. I break these tasks into two categories: inwardly focused tasks and outwardly focused tasks. Inwardly focused tasks are the tasks that are focused on improving, evolving, or changing your skills and performance as a sales manager, while outwardly focused tasks are the ones that are focused on helping your team's performance.

The Cadence of Excellence:
Key Habits of Effective Sales Managers

Featured Technology: Sales Training Content

Not only is Factor 8 (The Sales Bar) one of two Certified 100 Vendor Neutral providers (Richardson Group is the other), they have won the AA-ISP Vendor of the Year award more than any other sales training company.

From the website (**www.factor8.com**):

Pull a seat up at The Sales Bar and get sales skills on tap. We've put Factor 8's award winning custom curriculum for BDRs, AE's, Account Managers, and Sales Managers online and available 24/7 on-demand. We are the only online subscription training that's focused exclusively on Inside Sales skills. We're known for getting new reps to quota faster and giving tenured reps new phone selling techniques that get same-day results – like 50% more meetings booked, 13 returned voicemails in 2 days, and nearly double the sales talk time.

We're also known for our Manager Training that teaches them real, tactical job skills like coaching sales calls, running pipeline meetings, conducting sales 1:1's and driving sales performance.

CHALLENGES ADDRESSED

- Shorten ramp time with custom learning paths.
- Get more appointments for BDRs/SDRs. Clients report two-three times increase in appointments.
- More deals with top-of-funnel skills for more conversations.
- Engage customers with value-based messaging and questioning skills.
- Differentiate with business acumen and customer engagement skills.
- Double time talking with improved voicemails and introductions.
- Improve pipeline velocity with the "closing for commitment" course that keeps deals moving forward.
- Better outcomes with questioning, listening, and opportunity qualification skills.
- Connect faster with prospects using tools that include script starters and recorded calls.
- Enable managers to provide better coaching with training and coaching toolkits for every seller skill.

KEY PERFORMANCE INDICATORS

KPI 1: Faster quota achievement.
KPI 2: Increased talk time and call backs.
KPI 3: Increased appointment conversion rates.
KPI 4: Higher monthly recurring revenue.
KPI 5: Increased pipeline velocity.

KEY CAPABILITIES

- ✓ Call recording library demonstrates the use of skills taught plus Coach-the-Coach courses where feedback is given by experts.
- ✓ Motivate sales performance and reward behavior with in-tool gamification.
- ✓ Prescriptive, on-demand learning and coaching with micro-learning searchable by topic and challenge.
- ✓ Enable career paths with pre-built and custom certification and learning paths.
- ✓ Engage reps longer with a deep sales and manager skills library with new content added monthly.
- ✓ Access anytime using mobile application.
- ✓ Reinforce knowledge with built-in quizzes and manager reinforcement toolkits.
- ✓ Interact via message boards, call uploads, and live events.
- ✓ Save money by transferring licenses when reps leave.

Sales Training Content

Imagine sales content that gets delivered in real-time as it's "needed" by the sales professional, in a way that the sales professional best learns.

One company, LevelJump, aligns sales training with pipeline stages in CRM and, according to their customers, helps companies predict ramp, launch products faster, and crush their numbers.

In the future, according to LevelJump, sales training and enablement programs will be "Pelton-ized."

You can read the full article here:
https://www.leveljumpsoftware.com/blog/3-ways-to-pelotonize-your-sales-training-enablement-programs

Another company disrupting the way people learn in real time is ConnectAndSell. In 2015, we filed a patent that *identifies a weakness of a sales representative based on a score; and is programmed to provide training content to a sales representative in real time based on the weakness.*

Chapter 20:

Customer Value Management for Sales

Your ability (*or inability*) to articulate your unique value proposition for your customer makes the difference between success and failure every day that your sales team presents to customers, and marketing engages via digital outreach. There are point solutions like ROI Calc, The ROI Shop (ScsaleX.ai uses The ROI Shop, so does Xactly Corporation) and others, but each serves a unique purpose.

The first page of the DecisionLink website (**www.DecsionLink.com**) does a good job of describing what is now possible, powered by AI:

Support your value hypothesis using these sales-ready decision link assets:

- Smart company brief
- Executive value graphic
- Value snapshot

- Value brief

- Value pitch deck

Featured Technology:
Customer Value Management for Sales

Building a "Business Value Assessment" or "Value Proposition" or "Business Case" or "ROI/TCO Analysis" is a lot like solving a Rubik's Cube without ever having seen one. Every cube (or account) is different. With numerous variables for each account, things can get complicated very quickly. Building the case takes too long and costs too much, among numerous other problems.

DecisionLink ValueCloud® is the first application and repository specifically designed to solve this challenge. Dig in and find out how we do it!

DecisionLink is familiar with terms such as solution selling, value selling, challenger selling, customer alignment, hypothesis selling, critical success factors, provocative selling, selling to VITO, the complex sale, and more. These are different labels and descriptions at the core of what might reasonably be called "high-performance selling."

The selling methodologies DecisionLink embraces, sales training they have taken, and effectiveness tools they employ revolve around a set of fundamental premises.

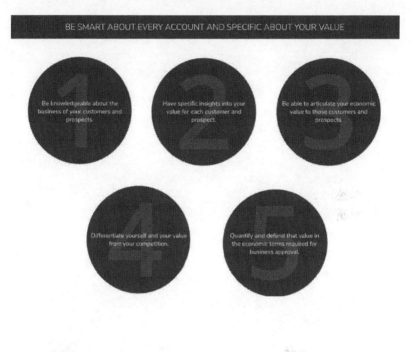

Customer Value Management for Sales

Aligning customer pain with unique value and economic benefit has been traditionally reserved for a few highly successful sales professionals within a company, or high-flying enterprise sales teams who invest in the tools, technology, and tactics, to deliver a compelling value proposition.

AI for sales will continue to close the gap on a sales reps ability to present a unique value (with compelling economic benefits). If the biggest reason sales reps lose deals is to "no decision," it's easy to see how AI for sales can improve win rates by 5%, 10%, or even 50% by empowering sales professionals with better technology to solve this problem.

Chapter 21:

AI for Social Sales

The purpose of ScaleX.ai is to empower average sales professionals with the tools, technologies and tactics to consistently perform in the top 10 percent. For those sales professionals who have invested in building their social network, this chapter is for you. For those sales professionals who haven't yet grown their LinkedIn Network to 10,000+, it's time to get to work! This chapter will help those who have 1,000 – 10,000+ LinkedIn connections.

Networking Has Changed Dramatically

Think back to the beginning of your sales journey. Do you remember when you were able to pick up the phone and really leverage your network in an impactful way? Warm leads were the norm, and you had plenty of connections who were happy to help in whatever way they could. But as time went on, your network helped you in all the ways they knew how.

You always thought that there might be more value in your network, but you didn't know where to look.

Leads became colder and colder until there were hardly any warm leads left.

Why is that?

Think of your network as an iceberg; most of the value is beneath the surface.

Many executives might think that they've exhausted their networks, but in reality, they haven't even begun to utilize the hidden value below the surface.

In today's world, our networks are larger than ever before.

With LinkedIn, Facebook, Twitter, and a multitude of other ways to connect, it's possible to contact almost anyone.

Despite this potential for networking, many of us only scratch the surface of our networks, allowing countless warm leads to go to waste. Because, while our networks have more potential than ever, they are also becoming harder to manage.

Imagine going through and organizing every one of your LinkedIn connections. Now imagine repeating this process for every one of their connections. What about the connections of those connections? Now repeat this process on different platforms. This task seems infinite, but that is the true power of your network, and it is possible to unlock that power with the introduction of AI for social sales.

Taking Advantage of this Change in Networking

Effectively leveraging your network is possible.

Luckily for us, there is an easier way to catalog our networks. Social platforms like LinkedIn already know who our first, second, and third-degree networks are.

So why aren't more people leveraging their networks?

Being aware of your network doesn't mean that you know how to access it. There are four main obstacles that prevent us from accessing the full value of our networks: identifying, prioritizing, growing, and network fatigue.

Five Main Obstacles and How to Solve Them

Challenge 1 - Identifying: Because of the size of our networks, we must process massive amounts of data in order to identify the value of a network.

The average executive's network has roughly 3.5 million data points, and it grows/changes daily.

But the average executive can only keep track of around **150 connections** (**https://www.bloomberg.com/news/articles/2013-01-10/the-dunbar-number-from-the-guru-of-social-networks**) in their network at a time (and even that's tough).

Solution: Through the power of AI, it is possible to automate the process of identifying and organizing our networks.

Given a direction, AI solutions can process millions of data points in your network and identify the most relevant data points for your goals. This allows you to see the full extent of your network, not just the tip of the iceberg.

Challenge 2 - Prioritizing: Although identifying your network is a step in the right direction, this information can be overwhelming and difficult to find value in without the proper focus.

It's difficult to know which individuals in your network offer the most value and which relationships you should focus on strengthening. And even after you've organized your network to determine where your value lies, how can you most effectively leverage those connections?

- If ten people can introduce you to a prospect, who should you ask first?

- If one person can introduce you to ten prospects, who should you prioritize their *"asks"* to?

- Which individual's reach aligns best with your desired prospects?

Solution: Through the power of AI, it's easier than ever to organize your network by important factors such as title, location, experience, engagement and much more. With this organization, it's possible to discover which individuals in your network offer the most value. You can then use this information to prioritize which relationships you want to strengthen and who you want to reach out to.

There are two major questions to answer when prioritizing your outreach:

- How strong is your connection with the person you're reaching out to?

- How strong is their connection with the person you are trying to reach?

There are thousands of data points that can help us answer these questions when they are properly analyzed. These data points include:

- How the involved parties know each other—same college? Same company?

- How many mutual connections are there? What other platforms are they connected on?

- Do they have similar titles, or are they in similar industries?

Analyzing these data points, in addition to many more, is the best way to prioritize your network for both relationship-building and outreach. AI solutions make this process possible.

Challenge 3 - Growth: Although understanding and leveraging your network is the best way to uncover its full potential, it is still good practice to grow your network.

Growing your network further mitigates the risk of network fatigue and leads to a wider range of opportunity.

But, how do you know the best way to grow your network?

- What events should you go to?

- Who should you meet at those events?

- Conferences? LI Groups? Etc.

Solution: Understanding the value of your network growth.

Let's say you went to a conference and met 30 people. Well, those 30 people likely have a massive second-degree network. So those 30 people might each know 200 people relevant to you. That could be the power of almost 6,000 people you met. Although AI isn't quite at the point of predicting who to connect with, this perspective can help you move in the right direction and get connected in relevant spaces.

Challenge 4 - Network Fatigue: No matter how warm your network is, it's possible to exhaust its value.

This network fatigue is part of what led to the disappearing warm leads discussed at the beginning of this chapter.

Solution: AI for sales allows you to easily keep track of who you've reached out to and when, while also cataloging their responses.

Having a full view of your network also allows you to spread your outreach throughout your network and only target relevant targets. With this level of visibility, it's possible to keep track of which of your connections are most likely to lend a helping hand and which of your connections you would be most excited to assist when the time arrives.

The Future of AI for Social Sales

AI will likely alter our approach to sales as a whole. Networks will become more important as marketing tactics become more commoditized.

The value of a relationship is only going to become scarcer. And, like anything, something that's scarce tends to be more valuable. There will be a shifting focus to find connections over cold activities.

The Marriage of Marketing and Sales in Growing Networks

This shift of priority will likely extend to related fields as well. Eventually, you'll be able to predict the value of your entire network and/or the value of specific people inside your network.

As a result, marketing will begin to shift its energy from purely promoting the company outwards to looking inwards, to helping the sales team grow their networks. Here are a few ways that we expect marketing and sales to shift as AI becomes more advanced:

- Marketing directing sales on what events to go to and who to talk to at those events

- Sales professionals regularly analyzing their networks to discover who they should focus on strengthening connections with and how to best engage their networks.

- Professionals of all kinds becoming more intentional with how they network

AI's role in AI for Social Sales

AI's purpose is not specifically around replacing the human.

Instead, AI for Social Sales' goal is to enhance the personalized aspects of your network and make you more powerful as a human. Although AI makes the process of leveraging your network easier than ever, it's the humanity of these connections that lend them their power.

Featured Technology: AI for Social Sales

How AI for social selling works in practice

Step 1: Pull a list of top target prospects (LinkedIn URL) from a lead/list provider like ZoomInfo Powered by DiscoverOrg.

Step 2: Provide FlowEngine with access to your social platform for 24 hours to run an assessment.

Step 3: Create unique messaging for each of the various types of influencers in your network: colleague, standard, "buddy" or exclude.

Step 4: FlowEngine analyzes your connections, your connections' connections, and more to determine the best path to your top prospects from Step #1.

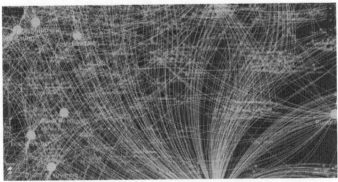

Network analysis, powered by AI

Step 5:   Classify your connections into the proper influencer type.

Step 6:   Empower FlowEngine to execute the outreach to your top prospects on your behalf.

Step 7:   Enjoy meetings with companies and decision makers within your top target accounts, with little heavy lifting.

Customer Quote: "Let the bots do what the bots do best; let the humans do what the humans do best," Chad Burmeister, CEO of ScaleX.ai

Conclusion

Reinventing and Retooling the Future of Sales Work with AI: A Moral Imperative for Sales Organizations and Educators

AI is one of the most significant and challenging trends in today's business environment, and it is thoroughly affecting the sales function. In this chapter, we analyze why the *data analytics – AI for sales paradox* will make the future of sales work more efficient and effective, while leading to a new era of *AI technology-guided salespeople and organizations*.

The Data Analytics – AI for Sales Paradox

Although AI affects multiple business function areas, its biggest impact pertains to marketing and sales along with supply-chain management and manufacturing[1]. McKinsey & Company estimates that AI can create across the world's businesses from $1.4 to $2.6 trillion of value in marketing and sales, and from $1.2 to $2 trillion in supply-chain management and manufacturing, representing more than two-thirds of the entire AI opportunity[2].

The main reason why AI tremendously affects marketing and sales relates to the growing dependence of such functions on data analytics. In fact, *in modern sales, if you don't have a data strategy, you don't have a sales strategy.* Yet, an important question arises: ***in what capacity should such data strategy be left to human intelligence (HI) or artificial intelligence (AI)?***

Data analytics, or the science of analyzing raw data in a decision-making process, has been identified as a critical skill in modern sales leadership and strategy[3]. However, the question of how to adequately integrate, pair, and leverage such skill with AI remains opened for sales organizations and educators.

While advances in computer science, big data analysis, and robotic applications continue to unlatch the automation of data analytics through mechanical processes and algorithms, one can only predict the expansion of AI-enabled data analytics.

---

[1] Miremadi M., et al. (2018), Most of AI's Business Uses Will Be in Two Areas. *HBR Online*, July 20.

[2] Miremadi M., et al. (2018), op. cit.

[3] Le Bon J. (2015), Training and Qualification: Developing a Competency Model to Assess Sales Leaders' Equity, in M. Zuech (ed.), *Handbook of Human Resources Management*, Berlin: Springer Science+Business Media.

The important question of what should be left to HI or AI then leads to what I call the *data analytics-AI for sales paradox.* Indeed, on one hand, data analytics skills can make a big difference in successful sales leadership and strategies. On the other hand, due to the cognitive limitations of the human brain in information processing, AI-enabled data analytics will surpass human-enabled data analytics.

No offense to the human species, but this is purely speed and volume physics. Speed wise, depending on the type of neuron and the importance of a quick response, brain neurons may travel 100 meters per second. In computers, signals may travel at the speed of light or 299,792 kilometers per second.

Volume wise, the human brain remains confined into the limited space of the cranium. However, cloud computing operates from growing and large-sized data centers where substantial amount of information can be managed. In the past, humanity built ports, train stations, and airports to communicate and trade. Today, humanity builds data centers. Interestingly, there are now more data centers worldwide (i.e., 509,147)[4] than plant species (i.e., 391,000). Subsequently, if we add to the human brain's speed and volume limitations, the ones of memory, perception, bias, resistance to change, fatigue, disorders, etc., we are better off supplementing the brain with AI capabilities rather than working without AI, especially in sales.

---

[4] Emerson Network Power (2011), *The State of Data Centers*, Emerson.

AI and the Future of Sales Work Efficiency and Effectiveness

When it comes to the future of sales work, the question of what should be left to HI or AI can be analyzed through the lenses of work efficiency and effectiveness, and organizational design and capabilities.

The sales function implies the management of many potential inefficiencies (e.g., hiring and training the right sales representatives, identifying and prioritizing the most promising customers, adopting and leveraging proper sales technologies, etc.) which challenge sales organizations' efficiency and effectiveness.

Efficiency refers to the *how*, or doing things right to achieve maximum productivity with minimum wasted time, effort, and expense (e.g., how to increase the number of phone calls a day). *Effectiveness* refers to the *what*, or doing the right things to achieve the desired goals and intended results (e.g., what are customers most likely to buy).

Thankfully, the very nature of AI is about solving operational problems of efficiency and effectiveness.

That is to say, through deep learning from big data analytics and the quick recognition of patterns, AI incorporates the power of many and compiles at a massive scale what works and what does not. AI reduces uncertainty and the likelihood of mistakes, brings experience to the inexperienced, and thus makes the average individual better, despite the law of physics limiting his or her brain's speed and volume capabilities.

Consequently, AI does two very important things to the human brain. AI *assists* and AI *augments*.

Interestingly, *assistance* suits *efficiency*, namely doing things right to achieve maximum productivity with minimum wasted time, effort, and expense (e.g., increasing the number of phone calls a day leveraging ScaleX.ai). Further, *augmentation* suits *effectiveness*, namely doing the right things to achieve the desired goals, and intended results (e.g., calling first the customers who are most likely to buy leveraging Salesforce Einstein).

Hence, when it comes to sales, it is important to envision AI in terms of *AI-assisted efficiency* and *AI-augmented effectiveness*[5].

We can now focus on the future of sales work where *AI-assisted efficiency* and *AI-augmented effectiveness* are at play for sales related tasks and activities.

Broadly defined as the focus of effort on an array of activities and tasks toward the accomplishment of an objective, work implies four important elements: effort, tasks, activities, and objective. We define a *task* as a piece of work that needs to be performed (e.g., making a phone call), and an *activity* as the exertion of an action (e.g., prospecting) which may comprise multiple tasks.

To perform adequately at their tasks and activities, salespeople also need skills, defined as proficiency in performance. Yet, there are two types of skills, hard skills and soft skills. *Hard skills* are technical-based abilities and

---

[5] Le Bon J. (2018), Artificial Intelligence, Sales Efficiency & Sales Effectiveness, *AA-ISP American Association of Inside Sales Professionals Artificial Intelligence Summit*, May, Chicago, Illinois, U.S.A

knowledge related to procedures (e.g., using CRM software). *Soft skills* are people-based abilities and qualities related to interpersonal interactions (e.g., active listening).

In addition to salespeople's tasks, activities, and hard and soft skills, we need to build on organizational design and capabilities to understand better what should be left to HI or AI. Overall, sales tasks and activities are integrated within an organization's *process, structure, people,* and *technology* that hopefully reflect and align with the strategy[6].

Although Vendor Neutral Certified 100 Landscape covers twenty sales-related activities (see Table 1), it is important to complement such framework with research-based sales tasks, activities, and hard and soft skills to more specifically describe and understand how AI affects the future of sales work.

---

[6] Le Bon J. (2018), The Role of Artificial Intelligence in the Future of Sales, *AMA American Marketing Association Faculty Consortium*, New Horizons in Selling and Sales Management, August, Boston, Massachusetts, U.S.A.

Table 1
Vendor Neutral Certified 100 Landscape and Activities

Vendor Neutral Certified 100 Landscape
1: Lead / List Building
2: Pricing & Configuration
3: Scheduling
4: Quota & Territory Management
5: Account Targeting & Go-To-Market
6: Prospect Engagement
7: Sales Enablement / Content Management
8: Outbound Prospecting / Agent-Assisted
9: Account & Opportunity Planning / Management
10: Video Selling
11: Lead Engagement
12: eSignature
13: Sales Assessments
14: Mobile Selling & Content Engagement
15: Sales Compensation
16: Knowledge Sharing
17: Conversation Intelligence
18: Skills Development & Reinforcement
19: Sales Training Content
20: Value Selling

In their research on *A Contemporary Taxonomy of Sales Positions*, Moncrief, Marshall, and Lassk (2006)[7], developed an empirically generated sales position taxonomy based on changing selling activities and strategies. They identify a set of 105 activities factor analyzed into 12 dimensions of selling, and 6 clusters of sales jobs. To explore further the tasks AI may handle, we complement this analysis with Antonio and Glenn-Anderson's (2018)[8] *Sales Ex Machina* book where the authors provide a list of 27 B2B sales tasks, and identify 10 of them machines can handle[9].

However, such frameworks do not approach the sales role in terms of hard and soft skills, which I believe are important to have a better understanding on how AI truly affects the sales work. This leads to propose a more comprehensive classification of the sales work based on sales related *foundational activities, intrinsic tasks, peripheral activities,* along with *hard* and *soft skills.* See Table 2 (a), (b), and (c).

---

[7] Moncrief W., Marshall G. & Lassk F., (2006), A Contemporary Taxonomy of Sales Positions, *Journal of Personal Selling & Sales Management*, 26 (1), 55-65.

[8] Antonio V. & Glenn-Anderson J. (2018), *Sales Ex Machina*, Alpharetta GA: Sellinger Group.

[9] Antonio V. & Glenn-Anderson J. (2018) specific tasks that can be handled by machine: 1. Sort through new leads; 2. Prioritize leads; 4. Send follow-up emails; 5. Respond to general inquiries via phone or online; 8. Generate a weekly report; 9. Set up customer meetings; 11. Make plane, hotel, and car reservations; 16. Develop a customized proposal; 19. RFM analysis; 20. Submit proposal pricing.

Table 2 (a) Sales Skills, Activities, Tasks, and AI

Sales Skills, Activities & Tasks	Hard Skills	Soft Skills	AI-Assisted Efficiency	AI-Augmented Effectiveness
Foundational Activities				
1. Build Trust	X	X	X	X
2. Ask Questions		X	X	
3. Build Rapport		X	X	X
4. Listen		X	X	X
5. Overcome Objections		X	X	
6. Read Body Language		X	X	

(Adapted from Moncrief, Marshall and Lassk (2006)). Note: Usually building trust is seen as a soft skill. Yet in modern digital sales strategies, trust can be built digitally with a specific cadence, procedures, and digital tools.

Table 2 (b) Sales Skills, Activities, Tasks, and AI

Sales Skills, Activities & Tasks	Hard Skills	Soft Skills	AI-Assisted Efficiency	AI-Augmented Effectiveness
Intrinsic Tasks				
1. Sort through new leads	X		X	X
2. Prioritize leads	X		X	X
3. Cold call leads	X		X	
4. Send follow-up emails	X		X	
5. Respond to general inquiries via phone or online	X		X	
6. Call existing clients to keep in touch	X		X	
7. Deal with client emergency or problem	X	X	X	
8. Generate a weekly report	X		X	
9. Set up customer meetings	X		X	
10. Travel to visit a customer	X		X	
11. Make plane, hotel, and car reservations	X		X	
12. Collect receipts	X		X	
13. Fill out expense reports	X		X	
14. Update the CRM	X		X	X
15. Prepare customer presentations	X	X	X	X
16. Develop a customized proposal	X	X	X	X
17. Call client for clarification	X	X		
18. Check that all items are included in the proposal	X			
19. RFM analysis	X		X	X
20. Submit proposal pricing	X		X	X
21. Follow-up on the proposal	X		X	
22. Ask for the order	X	X		
23. Submit contract	X		X	
24. Negotiate aspects of the contract		X		
25. Get final approval from legal	X	X		
26. Get the necessary signatures	X	X		
27. Close the sale		X		

(Adapted from Antonio and Glenn-Anderson (2018))

Table 2 (c) Sales Skills, Activities, Tasks, and AI

Sales Skills, Activities & Tasks	Hard Skills	Soft Skills	AI-Assisted Efficiency	AI-Augmented Effectiveness
Peripheral Activities				
1. Work with Key Accounts		X		
2. ID Person in Authority		X	X	
3. Plan Selling Activities	X	X	X	X
4. Call on Multiple Individuals	X	X	X	X
5. Help Clients Plan	X	X	X	
6. Train Customers with Product	X	X	X	
7. Introduce New Products	X	X		
8. Entertain Customers		X	X	
9. Train New Sales Reps	X	X		
10. Mentor Junior Sales Reps	X	X		
11. Attend Sales Meetings	X			
12. Attend Training Sessions		X	X	X
13. Learn About Products	X	X	X	

(Adapted from Moncrief, Marshall and Lassk (2006))

Through a deeper analysis of sales activities, tasks, and hard and soft skills, we see that AI can, and will, handle at a large scale the sales work, for the good.

Because the sales role involves of lot of hard skills, by definition, such technical-based abilities and procedures can be automated and assisted by AI, especially for sales related *intrinsic tasks* (e.g., updating the CRM with dictated notes and reminders to follow up efficiently with customers leveraging Chorus.ai). Moreover, several soft skills pertaining to sales related *foundational activities* and *peripheral activities* can not only be assisted, but also augmented by AI (e.g., building rapport and calling on multiple individuals effectively with profiled and customized presentations leveraging JOY.ai).

AI-assisted efficiency definitely helps salespeople do things right while achieving maximum productivity with minimum wasted time, effort, and expense. *AI-augmented effectiveness* clearly helps salespeople do the right things while achieving the desired goals, and intended results.

As a consequence, a brief look at what AI may not handle (where there is no 'X' in the Table) quickly helps us understand that AI will provide more time to salespeople to focus on higher value sales work. This may comprise critical sales tasks and activities such as *interacting with customers, making sure the proposals fit the objectives, negotiating contracts, on-boarding key stakeholders, closing the deal, working with key accounts, introducing new products, entertaining customers, mentoring other salespeople, etc.*

Further, by combining Vendor Neutral Certified 100 Landscape 20 sales related activities, with the lenses of *AI-assisted efficiency* and *AI-augmented effectiveness*, we believe AI can, and will, affect broadly the sales work, and improve an organizations' *process, structure, people,* and *technology,* thus design, capabilities, and strategy.

This leads to propose the concept of *AI-embedded sales work* and suggest that sales is evolving from human-guided sales to technology-automated sales, and now to technology-guided sales.

Human-guided sales — prior to late 1990s — refers to traditional human-push-sales models that focus on customer visits and face-to-face interactions where sellers control buyers' information. *Technology-automated sales* — 2000s through 2010s — allows sales organizations to adopt sales force automation/customer relationship management (SFA/CRM) technologies, while entering human-pull-sales models where buyers leverage cloud-based and social media platforms to access sellers' information.

Today, *technology-guided sales* is emerging as an era of technology-push-sales models where AI not only automates, but also assists and augments salespeople and sales organizations in a pervasive way. By *technology-guided sales*, and per the concept of technology-guided missiles, we mean that the technology autonomously and adaptively provides guidance and direction to the salesperson's tasks and activities by assisting and augmenting his or her brain capabilities for a more efficient and effective role.

When it comes to AI in sales work, we call this new era *AI technology-guided sales organizations* and *AI-technology guided salespeople*[10]. See Table 3 (along with Table 1) where the numbers represent where the Vendor Neutral Certified 100 Landscape 20 sales related activities fit.

Table 3
AI-Embedded and Technology-Guided Sales Work

AI-Embedded Sales Work		AI Technology-Guided Sales Organizations			
		People	Structure	Process	
				Sales Engagement	Customer Engagement
AI-Technology Guided Salespeople	AI-Augmented Effectiveness	4; 5; 7; 9; 10; 13; 15; 16; 18; 19	7; 9; 13; 15	5; 6; 10; 14; 17; 20	5; 6; 10; 14; 16; 17; 20
	AI-Assisted Efficiency	1; 3; 4; 8; 11; 12	4	2; 8; 11	2; 3; 8; 11

---

[10] Le Bon J. (2017), Enabling Sales Leaders and Educators with Best Practices: The Technology-Guided Sales Organizations and Salespeople, *AA-ISP American Association of Inside Sales Professionals Enterprise Executive Forum*, October, Carmel, California, U.S.A.

Through a deeper analysis of Vendor Neutral Certified 100 Landscape sales related activities, we see that AI can, and will, handle large-scale sales functions for an organizations' better design, capabilities, and strategy through improved *process*, *structure*, *people*, and *technology*. Interestingly, and at the scale of the organization, most of the AI effects occur at the *AI-augmented effectiveness* and at the level of *people*, *sales engagement*, and *customer engagement process*.

This analysis raises important ethical issues that intrinsically relate to AI in sales.

AI, The Future of Sales Work and Ethical Issues

Nine AI ethical issues could be depicted, as portrayed through The World Economic Forum[11]:

1. *Unemployment.* What happens after the end of jobs?

2. *Inequality.* How do we distribute the wealth created by machines?

3. *Humanity.* How do machines affect our behavior and interaction?

4. *Artificial stupidity.* How can we guard against mistakes?

5. *Racist robots.* How do we eliminate AI bias?

6. *Security.* How do we keep AI safe from adversaries?

7. *Evil genies.* How do we protect against unintended consequences?

---

[11] Bossmann, J. (2016), Top 9 Ethical Issues in Artificial Intelligence, *The World Economic Forum.*

8. *Singularity.* How do we stay in control of a complex intelligent system?

9. *Robot rights.* How do we define the humane treatment of AI?

These nine ethical issues resonate quite well with the sales function. Indeed, AI can affect the *unemployment* of sales representatives by taking over some of their responsibilities and jobs. Consequently, if AI drives sales and business values, *inequality* is at stake regarding the distribution of wealth generated by machines.

Further, since sales entails relationship, trust, and loyalty building, what should be the role of machines in an exchange model based on *humanity*? Because salespeople are immersed into complex decision-making contexts, *artificial stupidity* may sometimes be at play when machines' decisions are made out of context.

AI systems can be dependent on collected biased, non-diverse, non-inclusive data which can result in *racist robots* issues in sales or management settings. Because sales activities integrate significant revenue and customers related information, data *security* is obviously a natural concern.

Evil genies unintended consequences may also occur if AI guides sales efforts in specific directions at the expenses of more relevant strategic or political ones. As AI systems are complex, the question of *singularity* and staying in control is important when it comes to who should own and run AI systems in sales organizations.

Last, because AI can assist and augment the brain's capabilities, how should we recognize *robot rights* along with human rights for example in sales compensation structures?

Notwithstanding the legitimate ethical issues and skeptical eye people have regarding AI, the *data analytics – AI for sales paradox* remains. Yet, if bad data and bad algorithms can make bad AI, the good news is that, at scale, AI still relies on human-built data and algorithms.

However, this reflection leaves business executives and educators with three critical responsibilities. First, equip salespeople with a modern and adaptive set of knowledge and skills to embrace the AI disruption; second, refocus salespeople's AI freed-up time on higher value sales work; and third, reinvent organizations' design, capabilities, and strategy for a new nimble future of the sales work embedded in the *data analytics – AI for sales paradox*. Because, *at the sales numbers game, AI wins!*

Joël Le Bon, Ph.D.
Marketing & Sales Professor
Faculty Director for Leadership in Digital Marketing & Sales Transformation
Johns Hopkins University, Carey Business School

About the Author

Chad Burmeister, Twitter handle: @SalesHack and @ScaleXAI

Chad is passionate about helping funded start-ups create a pipeline that's more effective than it ever was before! By combining best-of-breed sales tools, technologies, and techniques, Chad helps customers dominate their market.

Chad has been voted as a Top 25 Most Influential Inside Sales Leader by the American Association of Inside Sales Professionals (**www.aa-isp.org**) for ten years in a row from 2009 to 2019.

Chad is a regular speaker at conferences including SalesForce.com's Dreamforce, The American Association of Inside Sales Professionals, Sales 3.0, SalesLoft RainMaker, and LeadsCon, and regularly has articles published in *Fortune Magazine, Inc. Magazine, Selling Power, Entrepreneur Magazine,* and more.

Other books authored / co-authored by Chad Burmeister

Sales Hack: With contributions from over 25 of the world's greatest sales professionals of our time
  https://www.amazon.com/Sales-Hack-contributions-greatest-professionals-ebook/dp/B01451D9MK

Sales Hack, the Original 25 Sales Hacks
  https://www.amazon.com/Sales-Hack-Original-25-Hacks-ebook/dp/B01DCEMZXU

ScaleX.ai, Multi-Channel Sales Acceleration: Powered by Artificial Intelligence (Sales Hack Book 3)
  https://www.amazon.com/ScaleX-ai-Multi-Channel-Sales-Acceleration-Intelligence-ebook/dp/B079394BJT

Journeys To Success: The Tom Cunningham Tribute Edition
  https://www.amazon.com/Journeys-Success-Tom-Cunningham-Tribute-ebook/dp/B07F9YNQNT

I hope you enjoyed this book. If you did, please take the time to leave a review. It will only take a few moments, and you will be making this author very happy.

Connect with me:

Follow me on Twitter: http://twitter.com/scalexai

Friend me on Facebook: http://facebook.com/scalexai

Subscribe to my blog: https://www.scalex.ai/blog

In Memory of Barbara Burmeister

August 20, 1951 – December 12, 2018

Barbara Burmeister

Paige,
Barb's Granddaughter

I'll never forget my Aunt Barb. She was an amazing person with a real zest for life (and for red wine). When I saw her about a month before her journey to heaven in Madison, Wisconsin, I asked what was her biggest fear or regret in life? Her response will sit on me until the end of my days—that she wouldn't be able to see her granddaughter Paige grow up.

As my kids grow older, and my parents, and everyone in my life, I try to remember my Aunt Barb's words of wisdom—to take it all in and really "be there" to see your friends and family grow up.

Made in the USA
Lexington, KY
30 September 2019